Afraid of Losing Money in Cryptocurrencies?

Afraid of Losing Money in Cryptocurrencies?

Understand the Basics
Learn to avoid SCAMS!
Get ready to make money.

Stanislas Petel

Afraid of Losing Money in Cryptocurrencies?

Foreword

Cryptocurrencies have grown in popularity in recent years. Whenever they rise or fall, they make the headlines. Bitcoin was the first blockchain-based cryptocurrency and continues to be the most popular.[1] Following its success, over 10,000 competing new cryptocurrencies have already been created.

Cryptocurrencies are gradually evolving from a specialist area to a revolution affecting the world of finance and industry. Behind the hype, these digital currencies are delivering new advanced technology to solve some of the world's problems allowing them to be one of the primary reasons for their success.

Rick Falkvinge wrote:
"Bitcoin will do to banks what email did to the postal industry"

There are still many skeptics regarding cryptocurrencies, and I was one of them before researching them in depth. We must acknowledge that people have invested a lot of time and money into them.

Afraid of Losing Money in Cryptocurrencies?

We can realize their success by looking at a survey stating 94% of Fortune 500 companies' executives have blockchain projects.[2] Even financial companies like Visa recently understood that it may change their business and have chosen to accelerate.[3]

Important notice:

This book does not give you investment advice and will not tell you how to become a Bitcoin millionaire in 30 days.

This book does not recommend that any cryptocurrency should be bought or sold by you. Do conduct your due diligence before making any investment decisions. Cryptocurrency investments are high-risk in nature. Don't invest more than you can afford to lose.

I made this book to help new investors to be successful with cryptocurrencies investment.

This book's purpose is to give an overview of most of the basics you should know. Please note that several technical characteristics of cryptocurrencies rely on advanced mathematics and/or expert computer science knowledge. All this knowledge would not fit in one book. Therefore, to make it readable I try to keep a balance between being accurate and being simple enough to grasp the concepts.

In this book:
- I explain the formal knowledge such as definitions and main characteristics as well as informal knowledge such as social network slang.
- I will describe how to understand the value of cryptocurrencies.
- I present simple methods to understand how to invest in it and the scams to avoid.
- Finally, I will introduce the major Cryptocurrency projects and some growing ones.

Afraid of Losing Money in Cryptocurrencies?

Contents

Foreword II
PART 1: The fundamentals of cryptocurrencies 1
   Cryptocurrencies in short 2
   The Evolution of cryptocurrencies 12
   Crypto terminology 25
   Crypto slangs 29
PART 2: Cryptocurrencies value 33
   Value fundamentals 34
   Cryptocurrencies market value 36
   Top 10 cryptocurrencies over the years 38
   How to evaluate cryptocurrencies value? 42
   Fundamentals 44
   Meme coin & scam risk 52
PART 3: How to Invest 56
   The long market cycle 57
   Short time evolution 62
   Practical rules for investors 65
   Advance psychology impact 70
   ETFs and Funds 77

    Other ways to earn cryptocurrencies 79

    Investments scams 82

PART 4: The top Coins analyzed 89

    Introduction 90

    The Bitcoin: The King of Coins 91

    Ethereum: The Queen? 98

    Binance Coin 105

    Tether 111

    Polkadot 116

    Dogecoin 122

Part 5: Non-Fungible Token (NFT) 128

    Non-Fungible Token in short 129

    NFT are a risky and bad investment 131

Conclusion 135

Acknowledgement 136

Citations & Reference 138

PART 1: The fundamentals of cryptocurrencies

PART 1: The fundamentals of cryptocurrencies

Cryptocurrencies in short

Cryptocurrencies are kind of virtual tokens used for secure online payments, which are represented as entries in a globally distributed ledger system.

The ledger is hosted on a blockchain, which can always be increased in length by adding new data when new transactions occur.

Figure 1: Secure chain of blocks = Blockchain

The term "crypto" refers to the numerous encryption methods that protect these entries. Each data is attached to the previous data through some unique key making the chain impossible to modify afterward.

Afraid of Losing Money in Cryptocurrencies?

Transaction process

The cryptocurrency transaction process works in 4 stages:

1) User starts a transaction
2) The transaction gets verified on the network
3) After validation, the data is added to the blockchain
4) Blockchain update is shared on the network

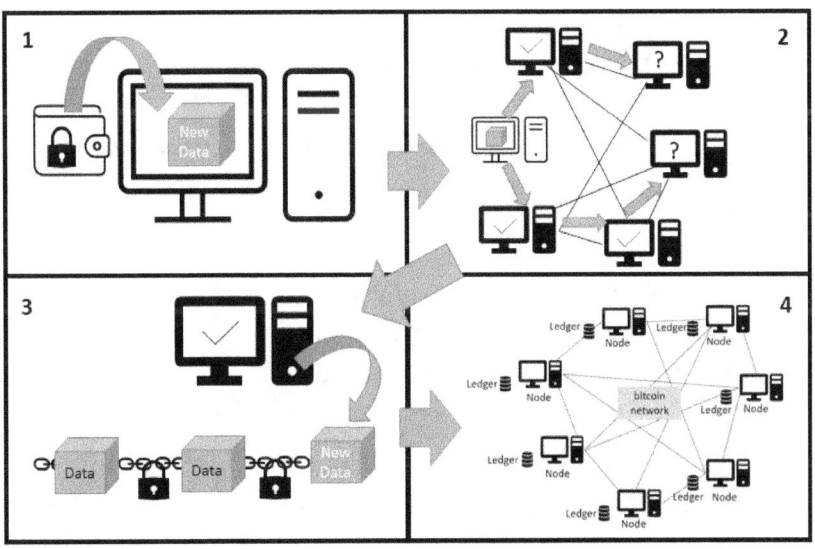

Figure 2: Transaction 4 stages

PART 1: The fundamentals of cryptocurrencies

1) User starts a transaction

Using a digital wallet and a computer connected to the internet, users can start a transaction in a similar way you would make a bank fund transfer.

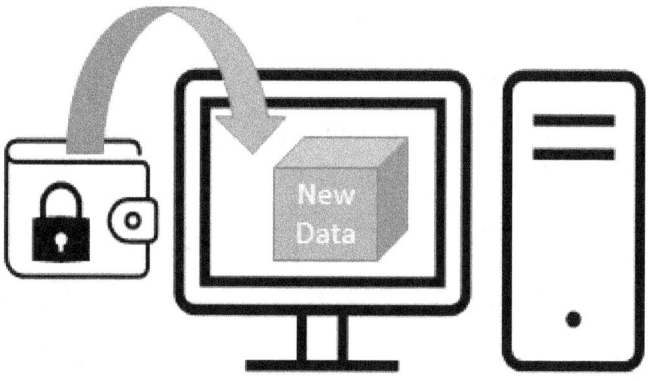

Figure 3: Transaction start stage

The computer will encrypt the transaction in a block of data using wallet security details to make it ready to be sent to the blockchain network on the internet.

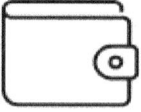 The digital wallet is a dedicated program storing the coins and encrypting them with a unique key so that only the owner can spend the coins on transactions.

Afraid of Losing Money in Cryptocurrencies?

Stealing someone else's coin is close to impossible as it would require breaking into the user's digital wallet. Those wallets are protected by some of the world's most advanced encryption mechanisms such as the NSA developed SHA-256.[4] Normal individuals or even pirate groups would not have the computing power to crack such security measures.

2) The transaction gets verified by the network

Transaction validation is enabled through the decentralized network made of thousands of connected computers. Each computer acts as a validator node. These validator nodes all have a copy of the ledger of transactions done through the blockchain.

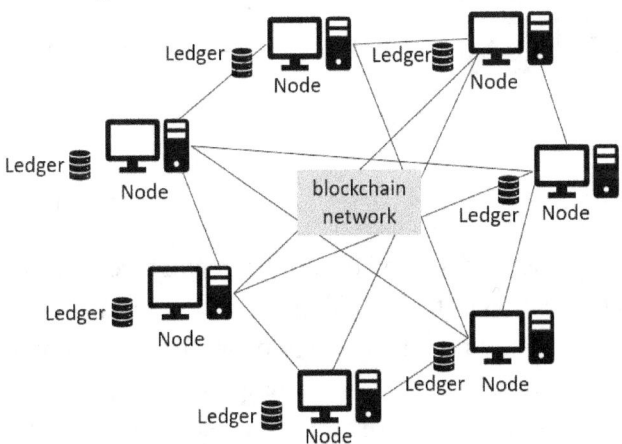

Figure 4: The blockchain network

PART 1: The fundamentals of cryptocurrencies

For every transaction, all validator nodes will check the wallet key authenticity and confirm with each other using some mathematically advanced consensus-based mechanism.

To encourage more validators to be part of the blockchain, the user pays some transaction fee sometimes called "gas". This fee serves as compensation to the validators for approving the operation and updating the ledger.

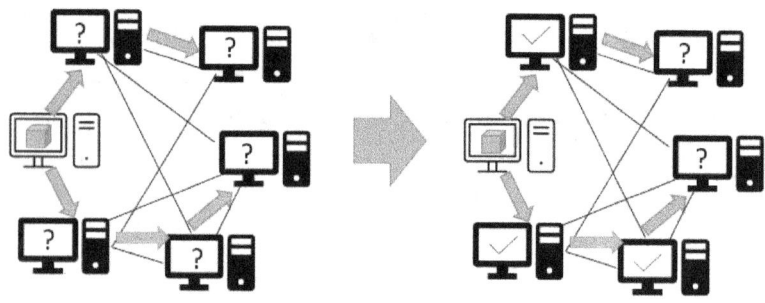

Figure 5: Network validation

Such consensus approval could typically be overridden only if someone controlled the majority of validator nodes, which would require a very large amount of computing power, literally thousands of computers. Thanks to this validation concept, it prevents fraudsters from creating counterfeit coins or forging transactions.

After a consensus is reached the data is ready to be added to the ledger in the blockchain.

One of the validator nodes will initiate the addition to the ledger by appending new data to the end of the blockchain.

Figure 6: New data is added to the blockchain

3) Blockchain update is shared on the network

The update is shared back to all nodes. The transaction is now final and cannot be altered anymore.

PART 1: The fundamentals of cryptocurrencies

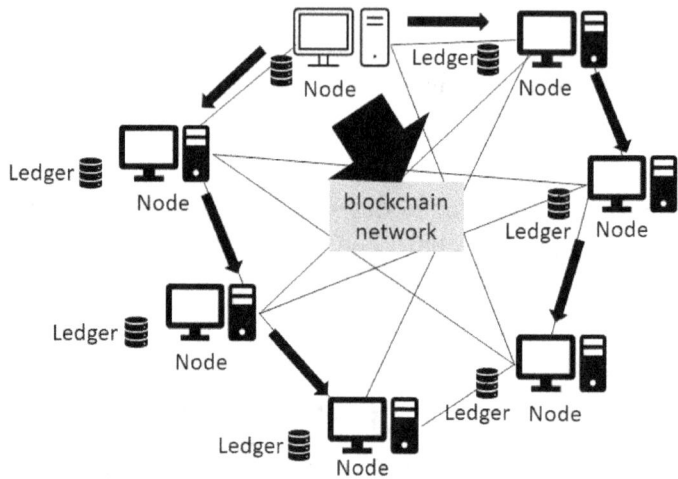

Figure 7: New data is shared with the whole network

The key benefit; Decentralized structure

For many users, the key benefit of cryptocurrency is the decentralized structure. It allows quick and secure money transfer among parties without requiring a trusted middleman, such as a bank or payment system like a credit card.

With a normal bank transfer, when a user sends money from his account to someone else, transactions go through one or multiple central servers before reaching their destination. After completion, the receiver would send confirmation which would go all the way back to the sender to finish the operation.

Afraid of Losing Money in Cryptocurrencies?

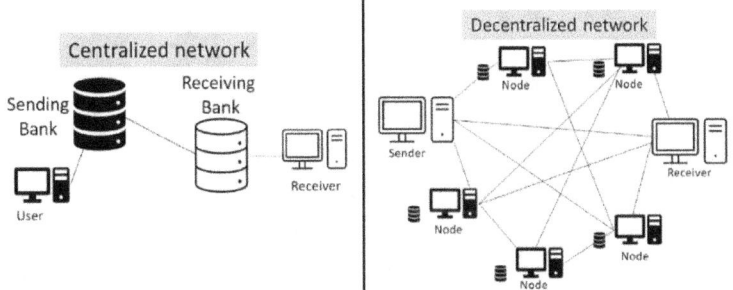

Figure 8: Transaction in centralized network versus decentralized network.

With a decentralized network, the receiver and validator nodes would receive the information about the transfer in parallel, the validator immediately confirms the correctness and adds it to their ledger. Decentralized Blockchain networks enable multiple advantages, including lower transaction fees and potentially faster transactions, on top of being safe.

There are some disadvantages though

High volatility

For regular investors as well as for payment, the high volatility can be a real concern. We regularly see coins gaining or losing more than 50% of their equivalent dollar value in a very short time frame.

PART 1: The fundamentals of cryptocurrencies

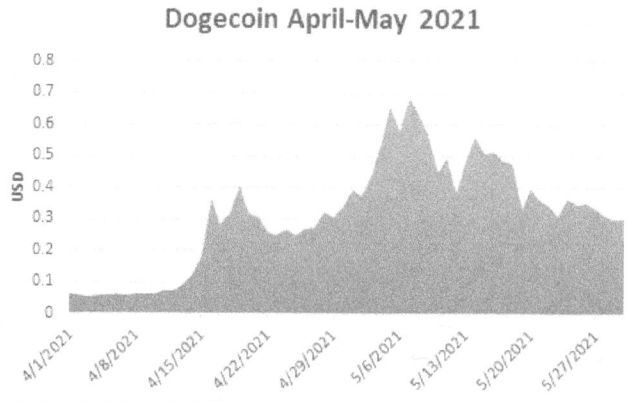

Figure 9: Dogecoin-USD value in April-May 2021 [5]

For example, strong volatility occurred on Dogecoin between April and the end of May 2021 with its value increasing by +1400% from ~$0.05 to $0.70 then quickly going down -50% around $0.3.

Such sharp movements are unheard of in the stock market, where monthly fluctuations of more than 20% are considered exceptional.[6]

It means any cryptocurrency investment will be a high risk all of the time.

Afraid of Losing Money in Cryptocurrencies?

Theft & Scam

 Some cryptocurrency investments are not worth it, and there can be many scams promising you a high return but leaving you only with tears.

We have also seen some issues with coin exchange sites getting hacked or suddenly closing down leaving complete loss to users.

Usual investment operators on stocks markets trading cannot be part of such scams due to strong regulations; it gives investors some protections which are not available for cryptocurrencies.

I want to emphasize again, be very cautious before making any investment. Do not trust random sources and *"do your own research "*.

PART 1: The fundamentals of cryptocurrencies

The Evolution of cryptocurrencies

Cryptocurrencies and blockchains have been on a constant evolution since bitcoin was released in 2009. Each new generation has been improving some limitations of previous generations. There is no official definition of each generation, but more an acknowledgment of what technology improvement is part of the new generation. Today we can distinguish 4 generations of cryptocurrencies.

1st Generation

Bitcoin

Bitcoin started the 1st generation with the following characteristics: strong encryption, decentralized blockchain, and the proof of work consensus. While strong encryption brings safety to users' wallets and the overall chain, decentralization was the real novelty compared to classical financial institutions, which have been centralized since the invention of banking itself.

Afraid of Losing Money in Cryptocurrencies?

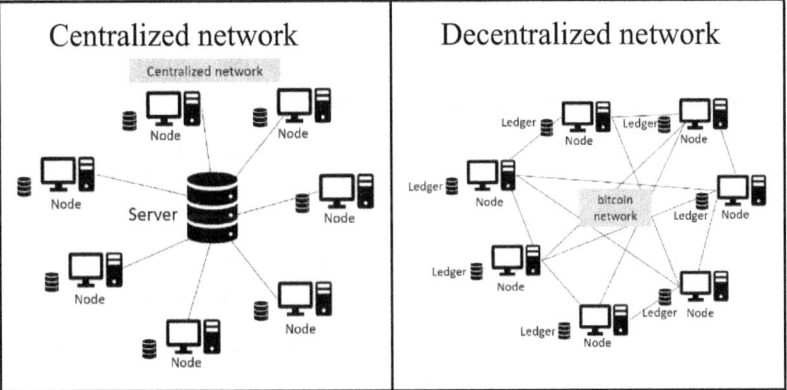

Figure 10: Centralized Versus Decentralized Network

The main problem of decentralization was on how to guarantee trust amongst users. In business, you could trust another party over time by asking for a guarantee or by being protected by another authority such as a government. However, for an online distributed system where anyone can be a member, it would be impossible to trust an unknown party.

The solution was to have 2 sides:

1) Rewards to validator nodes to do their work honestly.
2) Make it too difficult to defraud by overwriting the chain.

This is where the consensus combined with proof of work comes in. For the consensus, the simplest way would be to ask every node connected to check and ensure that at

PART 1: The fundamentals of cryptocurrencies

least 51% agree that the new transaction to be recorded to the blockchain is correct. Bitcoin is using strong mathematical models such as the Byzantine General's Problem to handle a consensus where some validators may be dishonest.

To ensure all nodes have enough time to communicate and reach a consensus, generating a new block of data is linked to a very difficult mathematical problem which all nodes try to solve in a parallel competition.

The node which finds the solution first (called the nonce) is rewarded in bitcoin itself. The node that creates the new block of data contains:

- The previous blockchain identifier (the Hash),
- The solution to the mathematical problem (the Nonce)
- The list of transactions to be recorded (Tx)

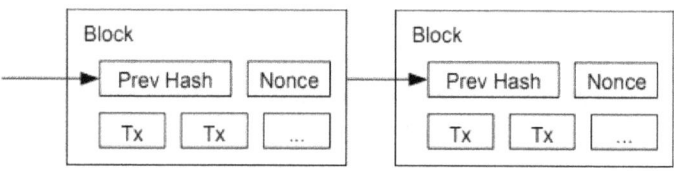

Figure 11: Bitcoin blocks [7]

The new block of data is then spread to all nodes as an official update. Following that, all nodes can try their chances again for the next block of transactions.

Afraid of Losing Money in Cryptocurrencies?

Side effect

As recording new transactions require solving a complex mathematical problem, it motivates validator nodes to have the largest possible computing power on it. Even with dedicated optimized hardware using GPU or ASIC, it consumes a large amount of energy.

Figure 12: Cryptocurrency mining equipment[8]

Some studies estimate bitcoin to use an annual amount of electricity higher than a country like Finland.[9] This is unsustainable from an environmental perspective as should blockchain replace the current payment system it would need to be scaled up thousands of times.

It also limits the speed of adding data to the ledger (the blockchain), with its current design Bitcoin can record 7 transactions per second which is much less than for example Visa system with 1700 transactions per second.[10]

PART 1: The fundamentals of cryptocurrencies

Typical 1st generation cryptocurrencies are:
- Bitcoin (BTC)
- Litecoin (LTC)
- Dogecoin (DOGE)

2nd Generation

Years later, it was realized blockchain could do more than only host cryptocurrency.

Ethereum launched in 2015, bringing a key innovation to the 1st generation of cryptocurrencies. It added the possibility to execute some code/commands in the Blockchain. The broad choice of commands can be used to execute operations on the blockchain in a much more advanced way than any of its predecessors.[11]

Smart-contracts

A key innovation with the 2nd generation was the possibility to automate transactions based on smart-contracts. Smart-contracts are scripts that run on the blockchain, which execute specific operations when predefined conditions are satisfied.

Afraid of Losing Money in Cryptocurrencies?

These smart-contracts are very useful for establishing contracts between new parties without the need for intermediaries. They are used to automate the execution of a contract so that all parties can instantly be certain of the outcome without any agent or middlemen's involvement.

Figure 13: Vending machine[12]

Like a vending machine

One can think of a vending machine as the closest image of a smart-contract: you see a price for a drink (the contract), insert a coin (start condition), and get your drink bottle (contract output result) without any delay or unnecessary interaction.

Using a smart-contract, users can trust that the transaction will be completed. Even with a new machine, users have full trust in the transaction.

However, the term contract is slightly misleading as it doesn't have a legal connotation. It simply refers to a computer program getting executed automatically when needed.

PART 1: The fundamentals of cryptocurrencies

Dapp

Smart-contract codes allow the development of Dapps or decentralized applications. Dapps would be like a computer program but instead of being stored in a server, they would be able to run anywhere on the blockchain.

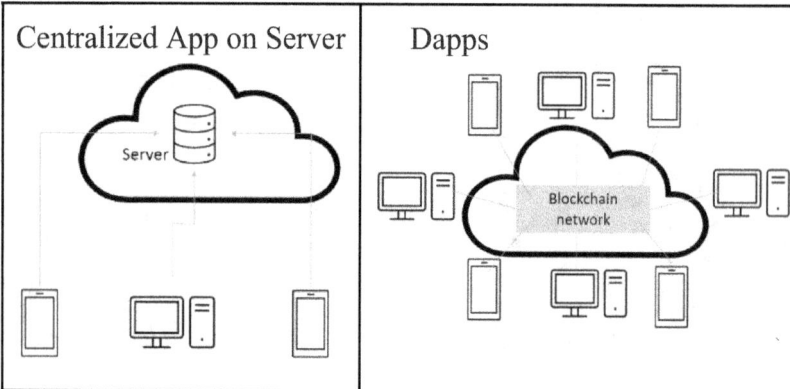

Figure 14: Centralized Application Versus Decentralized Application

Such decentralization protects it against the possibility of censorship or against any breakdown when a server or connection is unavailable.

Dapps are published on these open blockchain networks. Everyone can see the code, reverse-engineer how they work, and re-use them.

On top of this, the 2nd generation cryptocurrencies have also improved the basic features of the 1st generation, especially being faster to execute transactions and it rewards validation nodes by asking users to pay transaction fees. For example, Ethereum can process about ~1,300,000 transactions per day or about 2 times more than bitcoin.[13]

Typical 2nd generation cryptocurrencies are:
- Ethereum (ETHER)
- Binance coin (BNB)
- Tron (TRX)

3rd Generation

In 2017 some new Dapps became popular and led to an increased usage of 2nd generation cryptocurrencies. The increase of transactions created a slowdown of these blockchains as each node validation process takes time.[14] The speed problem became so significant that improvement of the technology was required, opening the door for a new generation of cryptocurrency to emerge.

Proof of Stake

A key improvement is the change of validation method from a proof of work to a proof of stake. In proof of work, lots of heavy processing power and processing time is spent guessing random numbers instead of only validating transactions. The new proof of stake validation method allows avoiding that time and energy waste.

PART 1: The fundamentals of cryptocurrencies

In proof of stakes, validator nodes must deposit some number of coins to participate in the validation when using proof of stake. While validating a transaction, in case a node fraud, and does not follow the consensus on the blockchain, it would lose the coins at stake. This prevents fraudsters from trying to alter the blockchain decision as they would be negatively impacted.

Figure 15: Proof of stake [15]

The only way to cheat the proof of stake is to deposit over 50% of all the coins in circulation. Thanks to proof of stake effectiveness, there is no need to engage large computing power to resolve the Proof of Work equation anymore.

Afraid of Losing Money in Cryptocurrencies?

Summary comparison of Proof of Work versus Proof of Stake:

Proof of Work	Proof of Stake
Validation is based on a global network of nodes.	same
Blockchain update based on mining = solving a complex mathematical equation.	Blockchain update based on staking = nodes have to commit some number of coins.
The first miner to solve the problem receives a reward as an incentive.	Validation nodes get incentives through transaction fees.
High electricity consumption	Low electricity consumption
Can be hacked if someone controls 51% of the computing power.	Can be hacked if someone controls 51% of the coins in circulation.

Table 1: Proof of work versus proof of stake

This change has been welcomed by the cryptocurrency community overall due to its benefits.

Many legacies 1st and 2nd generation chains are planning to evolve from proof of work to proof of stake concepts. Bitcoin lightning network layer or Ethereum 2.0 upgrade are some of the examples.[16] [17]

PART 1: The fundamentals of cryptocurrencies

Interoperability

A second key improvement is to have the possibility to connect different blockchains together. This can be improved through interoperability technologies.

Interoperability allows massive adoption as anyone could develop a new blockchain for their needs and connect it to a larger cryptocurrency ecosystem which allows them to distribute their service to a very large base of users.

Like a multi-currency foreign exchange where users can exchange any currency to another one directly, it allows exchanging Yen to Euros without having to do Yen to USD then USD to Euros. If this was not possible, users would have to pay fees multiple times.

3rd generation includes cryptocurrencies such as:
- Cardano (ADA)
- Polkadot (DOT)

4th Generation: the future

The blockchain community has understood that technological advantages are the keys to success in the cryptocurrency world. The 3rd generation cryptocurrencies are barely launched and already many people are looking at

Afraid of Losing Money in Cryptocurrencies?

what could be the 4th generation. Among innovations that are emerging, we can see the following key improvements.

Metastable consensus

Metastable consensus can be defined when the blockchain would not require waiting until the previous update is completed to be updated again. It means there would be no need to wait until the update has been completed and approved by the majority of nodes before it can accept new transactions. As a result, the time required to process transactions would decrease from seconds to milliseconds and could beat the best banking system today.

Sharding

Sharding is looking at improving the interoperability of the 3rd generation. New blockchains can support a multi-chain structure with a sub-chain connected to the main blockchain. This improvement is called sharding and it greatly increases overall speed and scalability to more users as you may have multiple sub-chains running in parallel.

Some new Blockchains are already becoming famous such as Avalanche (AVAX) or IOTA (MIOTA).

PART 1: The fundamentals of cryptocurrencies

Increased privacy

Another improvement area of cryptocurrencies has been pushing toward more privacy, such as limiting traceability of transactions on the blockchain and granting users further anonymity. Transparency of public blockchains means everyone can see what is happening, which is a good aspect against illegal usage but even banks today keep all transactions private, and most organizations prefer disclosing minimum legal information only.

Some blockchains such as DASH, Monero, or Zcash are trying to bring such privacy improvements.

Note there could be many blockchains claiming to be advanced, but it is difficult to judge them when they are still in development and have not yet fully launched these new functionalities.

Crypto terminology

As a new technology, cryptocurrencies come with many new words, here is a list of the basic terms.

Altcoin
Every coin which is not bitcoin and Ethereum is an altcoin or alternative coin, there are over 10,000 types of altcoins existing.

Block
Blocks represent a block of data registered in the blockchain. These data are the transactions recorded into the ledger as well as security encryptions data attached to it. As each block has a limited size, when a block is full it needs to wait for the next block to be recorded.

Blockchain
Key foundation technology of most cryptocurrencies. The name comes from the image of a chain of blocks of data with each block being connected to its predecessor and a cryptographic signature protecting from any alteration of the chain.

PART 1: The fundamentals of cryptocurrencies

Coin

The digital token or currency is attached to a Blockchain network. Some coin and Blockchain networks have the same name such as bitcoin, while some have different names such as the Cardano network coin being the ADA.

DeFi

Acronym for Decentralized Finance. A financial system characterized by the absence of any centralized organism like a Bank is replaced by the network of users itself to manage and record all transactions.

Dapps

Stands for Decentralized Applications. Computer programs that instead of running on a computer or servers run on a blockchain, As the blockchain is made of a constellation of nodes all running independently the system is said to be decentralized.

Digital Gold

Some consider bitcoin as the new digital gold as it can be stored, is in limited amounts, and would protect against inflation like Gold.

Digital wallet

A program used to store coins securely. Online ones are called hot wallets while offline versions are designated as cold wallets.

Afraid of Losing Money in Cryptocurrencies?

Fork

When a blockchain evolves but not all users agree on the changes it can result in a fork or a split of the community into those using the old blockchain design and those moving on to the new design.

Gas

User fees paid to use the network such as doing transactions or exchange of coins. The fee is usually earned by the validator. Gas name is mainly used by Ethereum cryptocurrencies, some others simply call it transaction fee.

ICO

Acronym for Initial Coin Offering. A common practice for new projects to gather funds required for their development. People would buy early coins to support the project as well as hope for profit as the value would increase later.

Market capitalization

The total amount of coins available multiplied by the coin value gives the Market capitalization of a cryptocurrency.

Mining

Miners are contributing to the network by generating new coins and registering transactions in exchange for a coin reward. This energy-intensive solution from 1st generation cryptos is disappearing in new blockchain generations.

PART 1: The fundamentals of cryptocurrencies

Node

A computer connected to the blockchain network and contributing to maintaining and updating the ledger.

NFT

Stands for Non-Fungible Token. Identifier representing the property of a unique digital asset that can be used to buy, transfer, or sell the property of the asset online.

Smart-contracts

A scripted program running on the blockchain made to execute a contract automatically when conditions are fulfilled without any intermediary required.

Tokenomics

New word made of a combination of Token and Economics. It refers to the study of how a cryptocurrency project works, its utility, and how the ecosystem understands its value.

Afraid of Losing Money in Cryptocurrencies?

Crypto slangs

Cryptocurrencies are very influenced by social networks. It's important to understand not only the official terminologies but also the informal knowledge coming out of these slang words and strange acronyms.

ATH
Acronym for All-Time High. When a coin reaches its highest value ever.

Bagholder
People who hold an amount of a coin or token which has lost all its value in the hope that it will come back sometime in the future. Can be assimilated as losers when said to others.

BTD
Acronym for Buy The Dip. Don't be afraid of the temporary dip and benefit from buying low to increase future profit.

DYOR
Stands for Do Your Own Research. The Internet is full of useless advice, most honest people would advise you to crosscheck any info yourself by doing your own research on the project.

PART 1: The fundamentals of cryptocurrencies

Flip / Flippening

When one coin is beating or passing another cryptocurrency in ranking. Especially used for top 10 coins where rank does not change very often due to high valuation.

FOMO

Stands for Fear Of Missing Out. People trying to follow others by buying recently famous coins in an already up market. Those people would buy too late and at a too high a price, ending up losing money.

HODL

Initially, it was just a typo for Hold, some people would describe it as Hold On to Dear Life. In both cases, it means keeping a coin for a long period whatever happens.

Lambo

Counting on immense gain to buy a Lamborghini... but usually used by those who don't have one and dream high or in a sarcastic way toward those dreamers.

MEME coin

Some coins were started as a joke following a theme such as a Dog for Dogecoin. Most of these projects are not serious and don't have utilities but sometimes reach significant value due to a fan base and (gambling) speculators. Serious investors, please walk away from those.

Afraid of Losing Money in Cryptocurrencies?

Pump and Dump
Short-term investors looking for coins to go up quickly (Pump) to sell it off with easy and quick profit (Dump). These speculators encourage others to do a group action to make it even more effective.

Rekt
Sound of the word "Wrecked". When someone loses a large amount of money suddenly to a barely recoverable level.

Shill / Shilling
Someone or a group promoting a cryptocurrency to have many people investing in it, which would consequently raise the price. Usually, the promoters would do it in their own interest to make a profit.
Note that in the normal finance world, manipulating prices in such a way is seen as a scam and not legal... but cryptocurrency trading is not regulated in most countries.

To the Moon / Mooning
When a cryptocurrency is going to skyrocket so high that its value would reach the moon.

Whales
The image of a whale jumping out of the water and splashing everything around.

PART 1: The fundamentals of cryptocurrencies

In cryptocurrency, some very rich investors or trading groups who by buying or selling large amounts make a big impact (sometimes manipulating) the market.

Some people define it as someone owning more than 5% of a specific cryptocurrency total or other by those moving several hundred million USD in one shot.

PART 2:
Cryptocurrencies value

PART 2: Cryptocurrencies value

Value fundamentals

Investors can be wondering why so many people and organizations are investing in it; Why does cryptocurrency have value?

Warren Buffet said during an interview on CNBC:

> *It's ingenious and blockchain is important, but Bitcoin has no unique value at all, it doesn't produce anything. You can stare at it all day and no little Bitcoins come out or anything like that. It's a delusion basically.*[18]

Such a statement coming from a renowned financial expert can make many wonders if there is any real value, but isn't it the same for the US Dollar, the Euro, or any other fiat currency?

The Britannica dictionary describes fiat currency:

> *Fiat money, in a broad sense, all kinds of money that are made legal tender by a government decree or fiat. The term is, however, usually reserved for legal-tender paper money or coins that have face values far exceeding their commodity values and are not redeemable in gold or silver.*[19]

Afraid of Losing Money in Cryptocurrencies?

As the US Dollars or Euros are not anymore redeemable in gold, what makes them hold any value? The International Monetary Fund (IMF) compares fiat and cryptocurrency to find them very similar:

> *Fiat money is materially worthless but has value simply because people collectively agree to ascribe a value to it. For money that is issued by a government, there is a guaranteed source of demand from requiring taxes be paid in that currency. For other money, such as cryptocurrencies, it only works because people believe that it will.*[20]

Fiat currencies hold value because users believe they are useful as a medium of exchange. In simple words, users can buy what they want with that currency. It is the same for cryptocurrencies. They should not be seen as just a token bought with the hope to sell at a higher value later like a collector's item. It is not only a tool enabling a medium of exchange, but also allowing more diverse services.

While some blockchains are purely looking at payment services, many others are serving multiple use cases. The range goes from automated contracts, owning digital pieces of art, online games goodies, or any application requiring a secure ledger with scalability.

PART 2: Cryptocurrencies value

Cryptocurrencies market value

Looking at the top 10 cryptocurrencies in August 2024 in the table below, we can see the coins have very different values. One single bitcoin is close to 60,000$ while some other coins are below 1$. Typically, cryptocurrencies are ranked based on their total market capitalization, not based on their coin price.

#	Crypto currency	Coin price ($)	Market cap ($)	Circulating supply (coin)
1	Bitcoin	58,432.00	1,153,038,071,516	19,741,875
2	Ethereum	2,613.53	314,201,134,189	120,284,052
3	Tether	1	116,674,806,700	116,885,176,708
4	BNB	530.81	77,415,508,517	145,887,576
5	Solana	142.36	66,427,878,785	466,319,674
6	USDC	1	34,778,272,428	34,805,541,378
7	XRP	0.56	31,571,018,384	56,113,081,096
8	Dogecoin	0.10	14,514,955,238	145,572,836,384
9	Cardano	0.33	11,894,178,975	35,620,786,512
10	TRON	0.14	11,743,955,546	86,952,481,080

Table 2: Top 10 cryptocurrencies market value [21]

Market capitalization can be calculated by the following formula:

Market capitalization = Coin price * Circulating supply

Afraid of Losing Money in Cryptocurrencies?

The circulating supply means only coins that are in circulation are counted. There are cryptocurrency projects with fixed amounts of coins, while others have variable supplies. For example, more supply can be added over time with specific conditions such as mining, while some others are reducing the number of coins by burning coins.

The concept of measuring value to a cryptocurrency focusing on market capitalization is very similar to what is done for stock markets. Some companies have more shares with low share value, and others may have fewer shares but of higher price.

The real value of the coin is defined by the demand and supply in real-time. When more investors buy a coin, its value tends to go up as it's in higher demand. Conversely, when more investors are trying to sell it rather than buying it, the demand is reduced leading to a lower market value.

The total coin supply is decided by the cryptocurrency project issuing it. Usually, every project is managed by either a private company or an open organization. In both cases, the total coin supply does not change without notice.

PART 2: Cryptocurrencies value

Top 10 cryptocurrencies over the years

Cryptocurrencies are very volatile. As new technologies are introduced, most older coins lose popularity quickly. Any cryptocurrency at the top this year may not always be a viable long-term option.

Top 10	2013 May rank	2024 August rank
Bitcoin	1	1
Litecoin	2	19
Namecoin	3	1083
Peercoin	4	930
Feathercoin	5	1678
Freicoin	6	7736
Terracoin	7	-
Devcoin	8	-
Novacoin	9	8065
Mincoin	10	-

Table 3: Top 10 market capitalization 2013 [22] - 2024 [23]

The comparison of the top 10 cryptocurrencies between May 2013 and August 2024 shows that only Bitcoin is still at the top. Litecoin stepped down to rank 19, while 5 others have fallen behind hundreds of existing coins in a nearly forgotten state, and 3 have even run out of circulation.

Afraid of Losing Money in Cryptocurrencies?

In traditional financial investment, you would usually see the notice: *past results do not predict future performance*. This is especially true for cryptocurrency.

The next table shows the top 10 cryptocurrencies' market capitalization evolution over the years. We can see that only 2 cryptocurrencies managed to stay at the top for a few years: Bitcoin and Ethereum. These are the ones that together give the tempo of the market fluctuation.

Rank	2013 May	2017 May	2021 May	2024 May
1	Bitcoin	Bitcoin	Bitcoin	Bitcoin
2	Litecoin	Ethereum	Ethereum	Ethereum
3	Namecoin	XRP	Binance Coin	Tether
4	Peercoin	Litecoin	XRP	Binance Coin
5	Feather-coin	NEM	Tether	Solana
6	Freicoin	Dash	Dogecoin	USDC
7	Terracoin	Ethereum Classic	Cardano	XRP
8	Devcoin	Monero	Polkadot	Dogecoin
9	Novacoin	Stellar	Uniswap	Toncoin
10	Mincoin	Golem	Bitcoin Cash	Cardano

Table 3: *top 10 cryptocurrencies market capitalization over the years.*[24]

From the table, we can see a few more remarkable cryptocurrencies. XRP is still in the top 10 since 2015 as well as Ethereum since 2017. XRP has been suffering from

PART 2: Cryptocurrencies value

a long-time ongoing lawsuit in the USA, but still manages to stay popular. Another remarkable one is the meme cryptocurrency Dogecoin which started as an internet joke. It made an unpredicted comeback, thanks to its fan base encouraged by Elon Musk tweets.

However, we can see most cryptocurrencies did not stay long in the top 10. Most of them stayed less than 2 years in the top list.

Also, it should be noted that the market has been drastically increasing in size. For cryptocurrencies that are reasonably well-ranked, they may have still gained value even if they are not in the top 10.

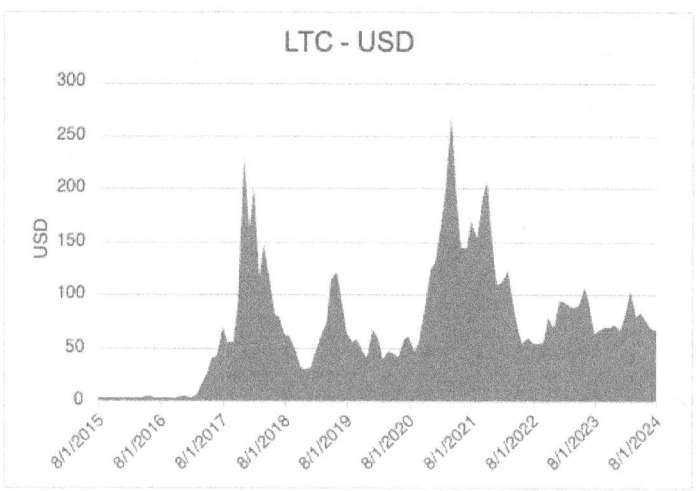

Figure 16: LITECOIN value 2015 - 2024

Litecoin has dropped from rank 2 in 2013 to rank 19 in 2024, however, its coin value changed from less than 5

Afraid of Losing Money in Cryptocurrencies?

dollars in 2015 to close to 65 dollars in 2024. Investors, which would have kept their coins all these years, would benefit from a 12+ times increase in their investment.

PART 2: Cryptocurrencies value

How to evaluate cryptocurrencies value?

Daily fluctuations are captivating lots of attention by their highly dynamic numbers. Some cryptocurrencies have increased in value by over 100% in a single day, some even reaching thousands of percent. However very often such high moves are based on temporary hype and do not last. The faster the growth, the tougher the fall will be. Only following trends and graphs lead investors into the trap of FOMO (the impulsive buying of a cryptocurrency by fear of missing out on something). Sadly, FOMO is one of the prime reasons for losing money in cryptocurrency.

What really interests investors is how to identify which cryptocurrency has actual higher potential. Finding out which one is already reaching most of its potential and avoiding overrated coins is difficult without practice.

Supply & Demand

Cryptocurrencies' coin prices rely on supply and demand. The more people are trying to buy it, especially where there is a limited supply, the price will increase, and vice versa. The demands should be similar to the cryptocurrency coin usage, however, today many cryptocurrencies are still new and have not spread widely, causing utilization to fluctuate. It can also be observed that increased competition among new blockchains is leading people to switch to more promising ones quickly creating waves in the demands.

Market predictions

Cryptocurrency demand cannot be predicted accurately nowadays.[25] Typically, experts would simply analyze price increases, link them to some related event that just happened as justification. Many forecasters tend to make overly optimistic price predictions, often because they also have a stake in cryptocurrency, and would thereby benefit from the higher prices.[26] Due to increased attention in news coverage, more investors would react or overreact to it, creating the cryptocurrencies' very high volatility. Some big players, especially whales and influencers, are trying to generate demands to control the price, but that can't be the way for sustainable investment.

John Biggs wrote: *Ignore the froth, hype, and FUD (Fear Uncertainty and Doubt) and instead focus on true utility.*[27]

To invest in cryptocurrency, we must focus on the true value. This value comes from the fundamentals of the project.

PART 2: Cryptocurrencies value

Fundamentals

Investors need to understand a cryptocurrency project's fundamentals to be able to see if it's worth investing in. The main aspects to look for in a cryptocurrency are the following:

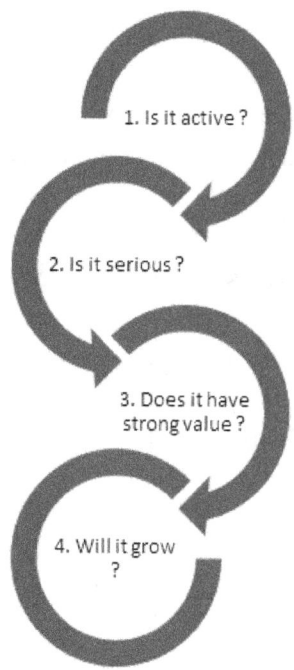

1) Is that cryptocurrency active?
2) Is it a real serious project behind it?
3) Does the project hold strong value?
4) How much value growth can be expected?

Afraid of Losing Money in Cryptocurrencies?

If the answer to any of these questions is "no", then we can stop looking further, and move on to study another cryptocurrency.

1) Project Activeness

While thousands of cryptocurrencies have been launched, some projects only live for a short time. To make sure any detailed research makes sense, the first point to check is whether the coin is active, which means that it is being actively bought and sold on some exchanges.

Websites such as coinbase.com or coinmarketcap.com allow us to easily see how much volume has been exchanged in the last 24h or the last 30 days.

Name	Price	Market Cap	Volume(24h)
Bitcoin 1 BTC	$56,879.49	$1.07T	$43,279,896,331 761,368 BTC
Ethereum 2 ETH	$4,141.74	$490.14B	$23,577,697,834 5,695,624 ETH
Binance Coin 3 BNB	$561.73	$93.61B	$3,341,366,625 5,953,636 BNB
Tether 4 USDT	$1.00	$73.04B	$97,308,749,852 97,233,752,747 USDT
Solana 5 SOL	$203.15	$61.37B	$4,357,553,753 21,558,671 SOL

Figure 17 Coinmarketcap.com Website View[28]

PART 2: Cryptocurrencies value

All top 5 projects have daily volumes in the range of several billion USD. Popular projects would easily be in millions or hundreds of millions USD.

Investors need to be very careful with projects which have low daily volumes. For low volumes, whatever the value of the coin is, it may be difficult to sell them and get any money back from their investment.

2) Project seriousness

Investors should consider the multiple factors to evaluate a project's seriousness. There are factors related to how it was founded, how it is planned, and what the development status is. If it's not a serious project, it's either gambling on a MEME coin or a scam.

Founding

- How long has it been since the start of the project?
- Are the founders and development team publicly known? Do they have any previous experience or successes?

Beware: a nice & fancy website is not enough to prove it's a real project.

Afraid of Losing Money in Cryptocurrencies?

Goal and plan

- Is the project goal clear and well explained? Do they publish details such as a whitepaper or complete explanation online?
- Do they have a development roadmap? (Great projects take years to complete)

Beware: projects claiming to be much better than others but refusing to disclose details on how they will achieve it keeping such details "secret", is probably a scam.

Development

- Have they been meeting previous milestones and deadlines?

Regular updates are proof of accountability of the development team. They can usually be found on the team blog, website, social network, or even news channels.

- Can we see the development activity on online code repositories such as Github? Is the pace regular for code updates? How many developers are active?

Beware: lack of visible progress of the development is a negative sign. Either the development team is understaffed and probably won't make it, or it may just be a scam.

PART 2: Cryptocurrencies value

- Are they transparently disclosing challenges faced by the team? Publishing 3rd parties audit?

Strong professional teams are not afraid of showing their challenges and demonstrating how they plan to tackle them. Oppositely, weak teams or Scams will always claim everything is fine to hide the truths.

3) Project Value

Intrinsic Value

After being convinced the project is serious, investors can dive further into the value it contains. Some key parameters are as follows:

Utilities
- What is the blockchain designed for? Which real-world problem are they solving?
- How much might people be willing to pay for such a service?
- How many tokens are already released? How many future tokens will be released?

Beware: Overgeneration of tokens would dilute and value created.

Afraid of Losing Money in Cryptocurrencies?

Ecosystem

- What is the ecosystem like, i.e., is the project open and connected to other projects?
- How many partnerships do they have?
- Does the token owner have rights in the ecosystem? (such as voting for governance or changes)

Beware: voting power majorly owned by a small group controlling the blockchain can create unfair situation for general token holders.

Competitors

- What are its main alternatives? How does it compare to the competition? What are the advantages or drawbacks?
- Are they already late to the market compared to their competition?

Extrinsic Value

Extrinsic value refers to the benefit generated by an external factor to the cryptocurrency project.

Marketing

- Does the project deploy strong marketing? Blogs? Interviews? YouTube videos?
- Do they have an active social network presence?

PART 2: Cryptocurrencies value

Community
- What is the community size? Are there any famous influencers among them?
- How many active nodes are online?

Accessibility
- Is the project available on multiple global exchange sites? Is it easy to trade?

4) Growth potential

Market comparison
- Compared to their competitors, are they undervalued? Overvalued?
- Are they growing in popularity on Google search or Twitter? YouTube?

With thousands of projects existing, every project should have competitors. They can be used as benchmarks for comparison.

Market movement
- Is its fluctuation correlated to other larger coins? Does it go up because bitcoin is going up or because of its own growth?
- Can you understand why it went up or down?

Afraid of Losing Money in Cryptocurrencies?

As we will explain in the next chapter, many cryptocurrencies are just following the bitcoin movement, but some have their own dynamics.

Other factors
- Are there any known legal risks?

Some projects, such as Ripple, for example, have been in trial with some countries. Another known issue could be if the main users are in China, with the Chinese government taking increasingly stricter actions against cryptocurrencies, it may seriously impact the project.

PART 2: Cryptocurrencies value

Meme coin & scam risk

Meme projects seem to be infinite with every new internet joke leading to a new one.

 The first Dog meme was Dogecoin. It was made as a parody of bitcoin, and following its social success many others were spawned following the hype:

- BabyDoge Coin
- DogeGF (for Doge girlfriend)
- Dogelon Mars (Doge + Elon Musk name + Mars)
- Doge Universe
- ...

And dozens more using various dog images.
- Shiba Inu (note: Inu means dog in Japanese)
- Hokkaido Inu
- Husky Avax
- Woof
- ...

It would be impossible to list all the meme coin types, but apart from the joke naming, their utilities would be lower than serious projects.

Afraid of Losing Money in Cryptocurrencies?

Scams, on the other hand, are a more important problem in the cryptocurrency world. While the meme coins are just for fun and can be a relatively harmless gamble, many scams are showing up. We can distinguish 2 main types of scam projects: the "rug pull" ones, and the honey pot ones.

Rug Pull Scam

In October 2021, a new cryptocurrency called Squid, inspired by the Netflix TV drama "Squid Game", stole 3 million dollars from thousands of people.[29] They were promised the token could later be used for an online game inspired by that TV show. The scam is that no game was ever created, and scammers just ran away with the money!

In a Rug Pull, scammers, through attractive marketing, get the crowd's attention with false promises about their projects. The false promises can be anything from very high investment returns, supporting revolutionary impossible projects, non-existing partnerships, or more. People join the Initial Coin Offering (ICO) to fund such projects, buying early tokens on some secondary and unregulated coin exchanges sites.
For some days, everything looks fine, and anyone can buy or sell those tokens like any project. Shortly after, the scammer disappears with the money on the exchange site.

PART 2: Cryptocurrencies value

Due to lack of liquidity on the exchange system, nobody can sell that token anymore and its value drops to 0. Those investors end up with a bag of coins that is not worth anything or can't be converted back into money.

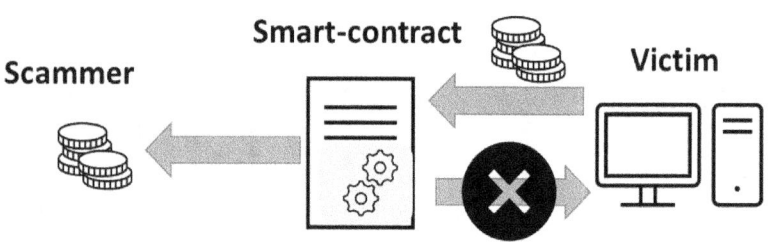

Figure 18 Rug Pull Scam Concept

Another Rug Pull variant can be created through technical manipulation. Blockchains where the buying/selling smart contracts have been modified in such a way that the selling option has been disabled through complex programming hidden changes.[30]

The Honey Pot

This is similar to the Rug Pull scam, but usually asks people to pay some money in small quantities to get a higher return later which will never come.

For example, scammers publish a smart-contract on a blockchain for automating a game, such as roulette or

Afraid of Losing Money in Cryptocurrencies?

guessing the number. If you send a bit of money and guess the right number, you get the money stored on the smart-contract as a winning prize.

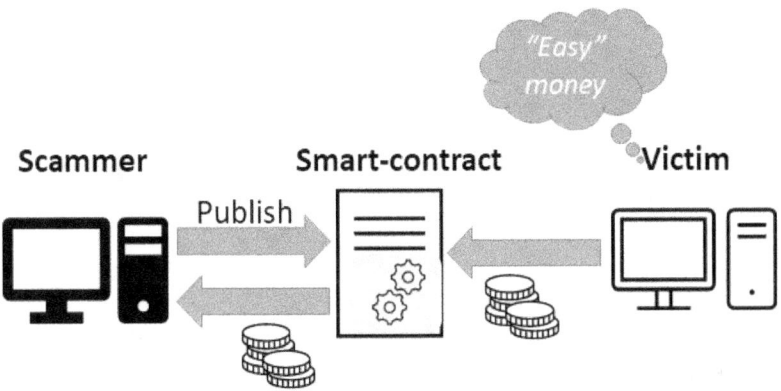

Figure 19 Honey pot scam concept

Somebody tells you that that smart-contract program has a bug and it's possible for players to cheat and win for sure. Users check the program code, which is fully available on the blockchain, and confirm the bug in the program.

Then, they want to try for the easy win. In reality, the smart-contract code is more complex than it looks. The user can never win, and the betting money is always stolen by the scammer!

New scam variants are created every day, so investors even experienced one, need to stay extremely cautious.

PART 3: How to Invest

Afraid of Losing Money in Cryptocurrencies?

The long market cycle

Daily values can have large fluctuations of 10%, 20%, or sometimes more than 100% a day. While these surges in value make the news headlines, investors should look at longer trends. Some long-term behaviors seem repetitive in the cryptocurrencies price evolution.

In the mid- to long-term:

- Bitcoin is driving the large market move
- Most alternative coins follow with some delay

The overall move pattern looks quasi-cyclic with 5 phases

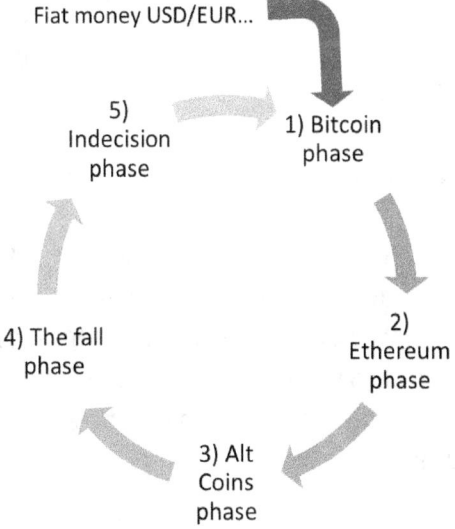

PART 3: How to Invest

The 5 phases

1) The king bitcoin moves up

Bitcoin moves up in value, close to its all-time highest value or even higher. This increase is gradual over several weeks. Bitcoin is the first to lead the move as it was the 1st cryptocurrency. It is seen as the most secure one by many investors.

2) Ethereum rises further,

At some point, some investors are willing to take their profit out of bitcoin and look for more profit. These investors start exchanging their bitcoins for Ethereum as it's the largest alternative cryptocurrency. Ethereum in turn increases in value and beats its all-time high value too following bitcoin.

3) Small cryptocurrencies rise quickly and strongly

Investors, looking again for more profit, switch to smaller alternatives cryptocurrencies. These alternative coins, having market capitalization much lower than bitcoin and Ethereum, are more volatile. The money transferred out of bitcoin and Ethereum can make those cryptocurrencies' value multiply, reaching a spectacular all-time high valuation.

Afraid of Losing Money in Cryptocurrencies?

4) The fall

After new peak values are reached in such a short period, market corrections finally happen. Investors trying to secure profit accelerate the market capitalization drop by selling their coins. Greedy investors, or those who invested too late due to fear of missing out on more heights, end up with large losses.

5) The indecision phase

The market would continue with some nearly flat phase for some time with limited up and down. That phase may sometimes last several months.

The long cycle lasts for about 4 years and is aligned to the bitcoin programmed halving mining return, as it creates a higher sense of scarcity on the market. However smaller scales with shorter duration sub-cycles can be seen inside each long cycle.

Exceptions

Some coins do jump up and down in value suddenly. One example can be in November 2021, while bitcoin was

PART 3: How to Invest

fluctuating around 60,000 USD, the CRO coin had a jump of 180% in 30 days.[31]

This move is surprising as it did not correlate with the bitcoin cycle, but they can usually be explained due to the following:

- Whales move, i.e., massive investors making large buy and sell transactions.

- Influencer action, cryptocurrencies are very sensitive to social networks, e.g., Elon Musk promoting dogecoin.

- Social groups moving together.

The CRO coin increase was due to heavy promotion with an advertising campaign featuring Hollywood actor Matt Damon, as well as the parent company of the CRO, Crypto.com acquired a major sports stadium in Los Angeles. Conversely, some cryptocurrencies sometimes jump in value for no real reason. In 2021, Shiba Inu had a 900% increase because some social groups thought Elon Musk was investing in it, which he denied being involved at all some weeks later.

In November 2024, DOGE value increased by 300% following Elon Musk's announcement of the Department of Government Efficiency (DOGE). Although unrelated to the cryptocurrency DOGE coin, the name was intentionally chosen as a pun.

Afraid of Losing Money in Cryptocurrencies?

Investors must remember that in classical stock market investment, organizing actions to aggressively influence a share just for speculation is forbidden in most countries, but cryptocurrencies are unregulated.

Cryptocurrencies with very low coin values are most susceptible to jumps, the simple reason is the higher the value the more difficult it is for someone to buy enough coins to dramatically affect the market.

PART 3: How to Invest

Short time evolution

Within the same phase of a cryptocurrency cycle, most coins will see their values vary up and down. In some cases, it can be very volatile, some cryptocurrencies may go 50% up or the full market may crash 30%. It's hard even for experts to predict how the market will move. Thanks to the volatility, short-term investors are looking for opportunities to make a profit in a timeframe of days to a week.

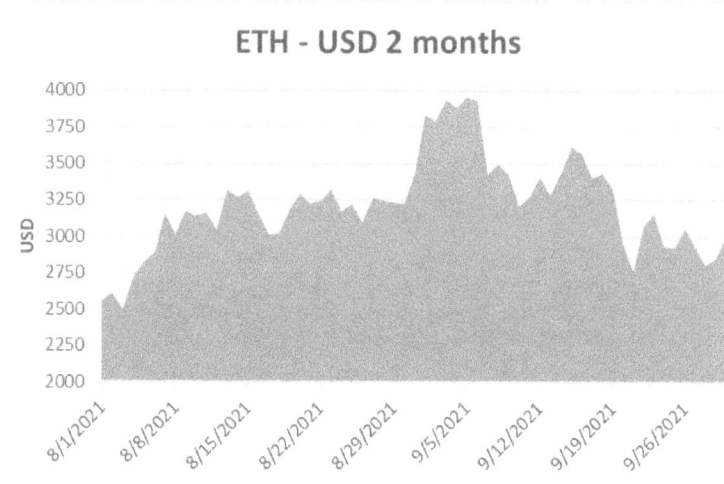

Figure 20 Ether price in USD during August-September 2021

While it started in August at around $2,500, Ether's price went up about 55%. The price stayed high for a few days then settled back around $2,750. We can see from this example that in the same period, some investors may have profited, but there is also the risk that others bought too high and may have made a loss at the end of September.

Day trading

One difference between the share market and cryptocurrency market is the definition of the day itself. Share market closes every day: the Nasdaq exchange closes at 4 PM every day or the French Euronext Paris closes at 5:30 PM (French time). Fixed daily closure time gives a break, a chance for investors to slow down, and see if what happened that day is in line with their expectations. However, the cryptocurrency market is open 24 hours / 7 days every week. There is no off time, no holiday.

The cryptocurrency market is always open and has the advantage that private investors can be active on evenings or weekends, outside of day job working hours. Investors have the convenience to buy and sell whenever the time is good for them, instead of being limited by opening hours.

It has the disadvantage that price evolution patterns such as candlestick become more difficult to read. The closure allows to generate graphs such as the following example:

PART 3: How to Invest

Figure 21: Day Candlestick Example[32]

Without any closure time and high price fluctuation, patterns may not be easily visible for cryptocurrency. Patterns may also change too quickly to have much meaning. Investors need to be careful.

Day trading is difficult for most investors. Many individual investors are looking into it as it brings the satisfaction of earning something today. However good investment can only be made when investors spend enough time analyzing the situation in depth. Being under short time pressure, it is very hard not to make an emotional decision when buying or selling cryptocurrencies.

Investors should be aware of the impact of human psychology on their decision.

Afraid of Losing Money in Cryptocurrencies?

Practical rules for investors

Basics of psychology to rule setting

Daniel Kahneman got the Nobel prize in 2002 for applying psychology to economic theory. He demonstrates in his book Noise[33], that any judgment, even the one made by experts, is not as good as applying simple decision rules. Most experts he encountered disagree as they prefer to trust their own judgments, rather than statistical unbiased data. His research proves that decision-makers would make better choices by just applying a simple set of rules to make their decisions. Expert judgment is only needed to define which rules to follow.

Simple 6 rules

Based on years of experience, here are a few practical rules to make cryptocurrency investments safer, and less impacted by psychological shortfalls.

Rule 1: Fix your budget	Rule 4: Define your investment timeline.
Rule 2: Diversify your investments.	Rule 5: Sell the profit
Rule 3: Keep some spare money.	Rule 6: Never rush an investment decision.

PART 3: How to Invest

Rule 1: Fix your budget

The first rule to set for an investor is "how much can you afford to invest? How much can you afford to lose?"

This should define your investment budget. Write it down and always stick to it. Whatever happens in the market, even if your favorite coin value drops 50%, do not increase the amount of money you invest to buy the dip. Never borrow money to invest more to recover a loss.

Most investment experts do not recommend investing more than 1% to 5% of your savings in cryptocurrency.[34] Remember that you may lose all your money as cryptocurrency is a very risky investment.

Rule 2: Diversify your cryptocurrencies investments.

Everyone is tempted when they find a new gem to bet everything in the hope of a 10 or 100 times return. Even if you are convinced one cryptocurrency is the best of all, do not put all your money on it. Most investors will limit their investment to 10% in one cryptocurrency, (or up to 20% if your total investment budget is small).
Remember cryptocurrencies are very volatile and even a promising project may face unexpected issues. The technical lead suddenly leaving the project, or Blockchain bugs leading to massive coin theft are examples of cases

Afraid of Losing Money in Cryptocurrencies?

that may lead to a large drop in value, and recovery is not guaranteed.

Investors should still be careful not to diversify too much either. 5 to 15 different cryptocurrencies investments are easy to follow up. 100 different coins would be impossible to check regularly. For that reason, holding too many cryptocurrencies is not advisable.

Rule 3: Keep some spare money.

The cryptocurrency market can have surprising moves. When some investors see a market crash, investors who have spare money to invest see an opportunity. In normal times, keeping around 20% of your money free for opportunities can ensure you will never miss them (while respecting rule number 1).

After investing your spare money, your next goal will be to replace that spare money.

Rule 4: Define your investment timeline and stick to it.

Every investment should have an expected timeline. Is this investment looking for a quick, for example, a few weeks' recovery after a dip? Or is it a long bet on a new project which may take 1-2 years to realize?

Before investing, one should set their timeline target. Not only the investment choice may be different, but also investors need to be patient during the timeline. Especially for long investments, the overall market will have up and down impacting price. When confident in a cryptocurrency's long-term potential, investors should never panic and sell.

Rule 5: Sell the profit

Investors' magical guidebooks always advise the "buy low, Sell high!" However, nobody can predict when the high will be reached until the peak has already passed. Applying Kahneman's psychology principle of setting decision rules means investors should define ahead when to book profit.

Based on target price predictions, it is safest to sell part of your investment when some thresholds are reached. For cases where you expect a 2 or 3 times increase, it can be selling part of it every time values have increased 20%.

For low capitalization and a riskier gamble, don't just wait for the 10 or 100 times increase. The safest bet is as soon as the value has doubled, sell 50%, then whatever happens later you won't be at a loss for that investment.

Do not be too greedy when setting your profit target, otherwise, you will be disappointed at the next market crash as some cryptocurrencies may not recover.

Afraid of Losing Money in Cryptocurrencies?

In the same way, well-prepared investors should have a selling target defined in advance to avoid any emotional decision. Wise investors know when they need to walk away and stop losing more.

Rule 6: Never rush an investment decision.

People tend to idealize an expert investor as a genius who looks at a graph on a screen and immediately makes a large action to buy one coin instead of another. The truth is that professional investment companies will never do that. They would typically have a step-by-step decision process made to even prevent sudden actions from happening.

Being fast and rushing is not the same thing. Being fast means the investor is well organized to make his decision. Fast investors will follow their decision checklist diligently. they have set their tool in place to easily make any market data analysis.

PART 3: How to Invest

Advance psychology impact

Modern psychologists have studied human reactions for decades and found we, humans, are not logical when making decisions. Even less when money is involved. The excellent book "The Psychology of Money" gives a general introduction for those who want to know more about it.[35] This chapter will focus more on specific points directly related to cryptocurrencies that investors better know about.

FOMO

The fear of missing out is a powerful driver for cryptocurrency market overreaction. In case of good news published about a specific coin, investors tend to overestimate the news benefit when seeing the coin price already went up. FOMO investors will ignore indications showing the price is already high and self-convince themselves it should go up further. The further the price increases, it convinces more FOMO investors they should follow and do the same.

In other domains, the FOMO factor is sometimes called the herd mentality. The Merriam-Webster dictionary defines it as:

Herd Mentality: the tendency of the people in a group to think and behave in ways that conform with others in the group rather than as individuals.[36]

Afraid of Losing Money in Cryptocurrencies?

The herd mentality is also combined with the regret of inaction. People tend to think they will have less regret to act and be wrong than not to act, however, this is not true when someone wasted a lifetime of saving on a greedy wrong investment decision. Inaction (or late action) costs much less.

How to avoid FOMO?
1) Never rush any investment decisions.

2) Look back at data, especially project or market data, and decide actions only based on previously defined rules.

3) Do not change rules to accommodate gut feeling, which is most likely biased by the FOMO effect.

Round numbers bias

Making a price prediction for the future of a cryptocurrency is difficult as it relies on many parameters. The human brain simplifies the thinking of complex topics to make them more understandable. As a result of that simplification, the brain will try to align to the closest round numbers even if this is less accurate. This error of judgment is well known as the round number bias in psychology.[37]

PART 3: How to Invest

The rounding error price is quite visible on cryptocurrency user's discussion forums when some investors talk of selling a coin after its value reaches $1.00, while the coin is currently worth pennies at the time of discussions. Similarly, people may buy a coin after its price falls below a threshold.

The following graph shows, for each day, the lowest and highest price of the Cardano (ADA coin):

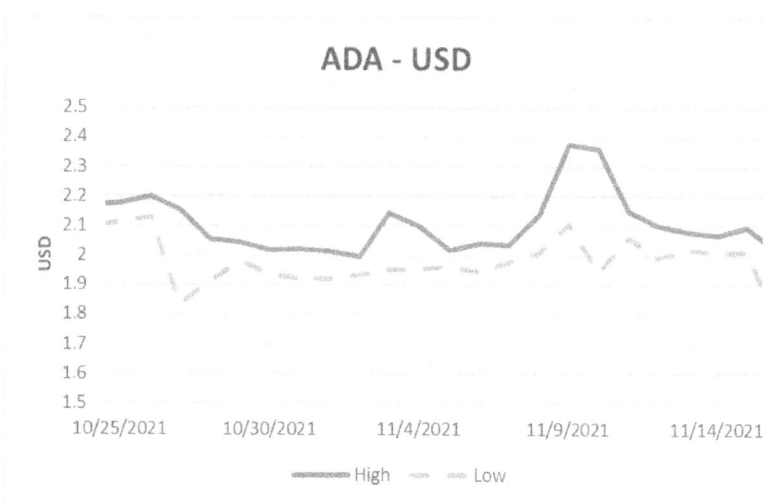

Figure 22: ADA Daily Price Between October 25th And November 15th, 2021[38]

In this example, several investors buy the coin just below $2.0, and some other investors are selling slightly over $2.0 price keeping the cryptocurrency price relatively flat over the period.

How to avoid round number bias?
1) Being aware of it when setting buys or sell price decisions reduces the error.

2) Avoiding it by buying or selling just before a threshold (e.g. sell at $0.98 instead of $1.00) may sometimes make sense but is not an irrefutable solution.

Social learning and confirmation bias

Investors researching a new coin, project, or technology about cryptocurrency would usually use the internet to find more information. While the internet has lots of information available, typically a search engine will lead to what is entered as a keyword. If an investor types out *"how good is coin X?"*, the search engine will return articles that include keywords good and coin X, leading investors to easily believe coin X is good.

The same mistake would happen if you searched the official fan forum of that coin X. Most likely people on that forum are supporters and will speak positive things, ignoring or minimizing the negative points.

It should be known that our human brain also makes the same mistake that psychologist Peter Wason named confirmation bias.[39] Naturally, our brain will be searching for information that confirms our belief as it's easier to accept and minimize opposite information. Even while reading pros and cons, the human brain puts more importance on the side we already believe is right and minimizes the opposite points. Confirmation bias can be dangerous as it leads investors to ignore signs a cryptocurrency may be a bad investment or even a scam.

How to avoid confirmation bias?

1) Investors should be aware of their own brain weaknesses and that they are potentially subject to bias.

2) Investors should actively practice the reasoning "for the sake of argumentation". Investors focus their brains to look for evidence of the opposite.

3) Instead of searching "how good is a coin?". Investors can search using negative keywords to see what negative points come out.

Cryptocurrency trading addiction

One last point to look at is that money is a powerful motivator for humans in general. Many individual investors look at trading for either making an extra income or dream of becoming financially independent. After a few trading successes which could be due to beginner's luck, the human brain tends to accept less and less failure.[40]

Afraid of Losing Money in Cryptocurrencies?

When a bad investment happens, those investors will look at more aggressive ways to recoup their loss by taking more risks. Some may reach the point where such investment behavior is self-compelled and not controlled anymore. This problem is the same one that psychologists define as a gambling addiction.[41]

Trading addiction, same as gambling addiction, has been a factor that did not only made investor lose all their money and take on debt, but even lead to social issues such as family break-up, or even suicide in extreme cases.[42] Investors should be very careful to watch their trading habits, especially what others may say about their trading patterns.

How to avoid trading /gambling addiction?
1) Investors should set reasonable expectations, limit their budget, and stick to it.

2) Addicted investors tend to hide their doing, discussing openly with family or trusted friends can prevent addiction from starting.

3) In case symptoms of addiction are already visible, Investors should just stop and get external help from a medical expert.

PART 3: How to Invest

> **3 Key Points to Remember**
>
> 1. Human psychology is a complex topic. Investors should keep in mind that being human, they are prone to bias and errors.
>
> 2. Investment decisions should never be made based on instinct and gut feeling.
>
> 3. Investors should always be careful not to make any decision that they may regret.

Afraid of Losing Money in Cryptocurrencies?

ETFs and Funds

An alternative to direct investment in cryptocurrency can be exchange-traded funds (ETF) and specialist funds.

These options may be useful for multiple reasons. Some investors are not comfortable with using cryptocurrency exchanges or are looking at ways to follow market trends in an automated way. ETFs and funds may also be accessible in some pension investment plans where direct cryptocurrencies investment would not be allowed. On top of it, investors putting more distance to their investments through externally managed solutions are more protected from the previous chapter about psychological effects.

Bitcoin ETFs

In October 2021 the U.S. securities and exchange commission (SEC) finally approved the 1st Bitcoin-based ETF: ProShares Bitcoin Strategy ETF.[43] Following its success, several financial institutions have quickly launched their own Bitcoin ETFs. Most of those ETFs are not directly buying Bitcoins but manage to replicate Bitcoin price evolutions with

PART 3: How to Invest

some futures trading or following some company stocks that are heavily linked to Bitcoin such as Microstrategy (NASDAQ: MSTR).

In January 2024, After multiple rejections, 11 Bitcoin Spot ETFs were finally approved by the SEC to be listed in the USA market.[44] Spot ETF means those can directly be indexed on the price of the bitcoin in real-time, however, this increases access to Bitcoin for many regular investors.

Thematic Cryptocurrencies funds

Investors can also see a growing choice of funds combining multiple cryptocurrencies together. Some passive only aims at keeping some mix of the top 10 cryptocurrencies such as Bitwise 10 Crypto Index Fund. Some more active ones are managed by either professional traders or algorithm bots. The Tie sentiment AI[45] or Napoleon-X multi-crypto AI[46] are examples of algorithmic funds offered on the eToro investment platform. They use not only traditional signals from markets but also other data such as Twitter trends to make active trade decisions.

Both options, ETFs and funds are investments for the long term. Professional funds should not be mixed up with the variety of lower quality investment signal bots available on the market promising quick success. These signal bots look at simple trade signals such as price trends, and not always proven decision logic. Investors should always do their own research before making any investment decisions.

Other ways to earn cryptocurrencies

Mining

The first bitcoin came with the concept of mining as a method to generate new coins. During the initial years when bitcoin value was small, mining was not so interesting. When bitcoin value started to rise, then the cryptocurrency saw a gold rush on bitcoin and the mining of other coins. Similar to the California gold rush of 1848-1850, large increases in the number of miners made the chance of making money harder. Finally, only professionals, well equipped with special mining equipment can be profitable and are still dominating the mining landscape.

A mining farm is made of hundreds of high processing computing units. In 2018, the company Power Coin Block set up one in the USA spending 251 million USD.[47] For regular investors, entering the cryptocurrency mining business is 10 years too late.

PART 3: How to Invest

Figure 23: Mining Farm [48]

On top of it, most new cryptocurrencies have chosen other technologies which do not require mining. Many legacy ones, such as Ethereum, are on the way to moving out of mining. Ethereum itself moved fully away from mining in 2022.

Staking

For some cryptocurrencies based on a proof of stake mechanism, there may be a staking reward. A large staking pool of users is needed to have a safe validation of the blockchain. The staking reward motivates the holder to keep their coins, and not sell everything quickly when the cryptocurrency value fluctuates.

Afraid of Losing Money in Cryptocurrencies?

Typically, a significant amount of coin is required to be eligible for a staking reward. Ethereum set the minimum stake at 32 ETH (which is currently equivalent to approx. 70,000 USD).[49]

It is possible to stake while owning a smaller amount if you are part of a joint staking pool. Most cryptocurrency exchange wallets offer such staking pool services.[50]

The longer investors stake a coin, the higher the return can be expected. Some blockchains would even have the option to have a predefined lock-in period. The duration can typically vary from a week to several years.

Compared with traditional banking, it's somewhat similar to having some amount of money locked in a fixed duration deposit fund where banks can use investors' money. In exchange for the deposit, Banks would give an interest rate. The longer the lock-in duration the higher the interest.

One key difference in cryptocurrencies is that the deposit is not only used as a liquidity reserve but also in the validation mechanism as described in Chapter 1 of this book.

One important risk with staking is the lock-in period itself. Longer lock-in looks advantageous in good interest return, however, the coin itself may have lost most of its value by the time it is unlocked and available for reselling. Not many cryptocurrencies have successfully grown over many years.

PART 3: How to Invest

Investments scams

Additionally, to blockchain projects' scams described in the previous chapter, there are more types of scams investors need to be aware of.

Common scam types are:

1) Social engineering scams
   a. Imposters and Giveaway scams
   b. Fake social network influencer
   c. Scamming email / Fishing email

2) Fake investments options
   a. Fake trading signals
   b. Fake whales' group

3) Fake intermediary
   a. Fake investment broker
   b. Imposter website & fake mobile app

Afraid of Losing Money in Cryptocurrencies?

Social engineering scams

Imposters and Giveaway scams

This scam usually starts with a message of a billionaire who says he decided to become generous to everyone. If you send, within the next few minutes, cryptocurrencies to a given wallet address he will return double the amount to you.

Sending an unknown cryptocurrency wallet any amount of money or cryptocurrencies is to be avoided. Investors should not even try with little amounts of money. Scammers always invent many variants of this type of giveaway scam, some even involving hijacked celebrities' social network accounts, or fake websites copying the sites of famous organizations. Statistics show the amount of such giveaway scams has multiplied by a factor of 10 between 2019 and 2021.[51]

Fake social network influencer

Cryptocurrencies are highly influenced by social networks. Some scammers try to take advantage of that by creating fake accounts and using them to manipulate the cryptocurrency market. Through the help of bots, scammers can automate hundreds of fake accounts to spread fake information on a large scale. Scammers do this to quickly raise or lower a cryptocurrency market price. This allows them to either sell their cryptocurrency at a high price or buy more at a lower price.

Phishing emails

As cryptocurrencies are online on the internet, they suffer from the same risks as other internet services. With their growth in popularity comes also classical email scams and phishing attempts. Instead of trying to get users' credit card or bank login information, scammers will try to find a way to steal the wallet security keys from cryptocurrency users. Users should never share their cryptocurrency wallet keys. The same as with banks not contacting their customers to confirm their credit card number, cryptocurrency exchanges won't ask users to send them their wallet security keys.

If anyone falls victim to a scammer and provides their wallet keys, all of that wallet's cryptocurrencies will be taken instantly and would usually not be recoverable.

Afraid of Losing Money in Cryptocurrencies?

Fake investment options on social networks

Many cryptocurrency investors are using social networks to find new hidden gems. They are looking for information about new cryptocurrencies which may be the next big success. From this strong interest, many cryptocurrency user discussion groups have emerged on internet forums, or chat applications such as Telegram or WhatsApp. We can see users genuinely offering their latest discovery but also scammers trying to lure people into scams.

Scammers may not always try to lure investors on scams projects, but instead, try to manipulate a cryptocurrency value.

Fake trading signals

Social network investors can be amateurs as well as professionals. It's common to see some investors sharing their market analysis to get feedback from other investors. Scammers may be sharing complicated graphs and detailed analysis results about exponential growth coming very soon to motivate investors to buy it.

They often come as a group with one scammer initiating the discussion, and other scammer accounts answering them, having a controlled conversation, and asking for more details or confirming that information to be true to make the audience believe their scam.

Any advice on the internet is to be taken with extreme caution. Investors should always do their own research and never rush to buy anything instantly.

Fake whale groups

In a similar way to the previous scams, some scammers try to invite people to join some whale groups (private chat groups) where whales are supposedly talking about their plan to make massive sell or buy investments. Such large investments would impact some specific cryptocurrencies' prices significantly.

The hope for easy gain, thanks to secret information, makes some investors fall for the trap. However, we have to remember the definition of whales. Whales are investors which can buy or sell several hundreds of millions of USD of cryptocurrency. They have no reason to be kind enough to share their plans with regular (small) investors and neither need regular investors to support their actions. Therefore, such groups can only be fake.

As those groups' organizers can't be trusted, investors should never participate in such groups, or believe the advice offered there.

Fake intermediary

Fake investment brokers

Either over email or through a chat group, we see scammers trying to pose as cryptocurrency investment brokers. Those scammers would contact investors and offer to buy some cryptocurrency for them at an attractive price, often lower than market prices. Scammers would justify their access to a better price by buying cryptocurrencies in bulk through direct access to project teams or similar hard to verify reasons.

The trick is that investors would need to use them as brokers. Investors would need to send them money and they would keep an account for you in their system. Professional scammers may even let you try with a small amount of money, and give you a nice return, just to convince you to invest a larger amount of money with them.

Investors should be careful before trusting anyone offering a better investment than the typical market return.

Imposter websites & fake mobile apps

The cryptocurrency ecosystem is still in its infancy, and some blockchains are quite difficult to access for regular

PART 3: How to Invest

investments. Honest market providers are competing to launch innovative solutions making it easier. Some are doing this by combining accounts from multiple blockchains or implementing better user features.

Scammers can sometimes go unnoticed and publish fake websites or mobile apps to facilitate cryptocurrency investments, luring users through early-bird discounts on service fees or promotions. They would operate for a short period and then steal all the user's money.

While smartphone apps stores would normally delete any scam apps, it is not fully safe as new ones can be easily created at any time by scammers.

The lack of cryptocurrency regulation makes it attractive for scammers as well as relatively lower risk for them. Scammers are very creative and active in inventing new ways to defraud investors all the time.

The general rule of thumb for investors should be to be extremely careful with anything which sounds too good to be true. Always do your own research before trusting someone else's advice.

PART 4: The top Coins analyzed

Afraid of Losing Money in Cryptocurrencies?

Introduction

There are 10,000+ cryptocurrencies and more are created every day. Looking at all of them is impossible for anyone. Fortunately, most are not relevant for regular individual investors, particularly as many will not survive.

This chapter aims to introduce the main cryptocurrencies which everyone should know about.

Top 2 cryptocurrencies in market capitalization:
1. Bitcoin (bitcoin)
2. Ethereum (Ether)

Additional remarkable ones:
- Binance coin (BNB)
- Tether (USDT)
- Polkadot (Dot)

Meme coins, while they may not be recommendable, are regularly making headlines.
- Dogecoin (DOGE)

PART 4: The top Coins analyzed.

The Bitcoin: The King of Coins

Logo	bitcoin
Symbol	BTC
Start	2009
Market Value	$1,156,564,762,000
Rank	#1
Technology level	1st Generation

DATA AS PER (AUG 2024)

Afraid of Losing Money in Cryptocurrencies?

History

While the concept of cryptocurrency was explored by some in the '90s, bitcoin was the 1st successful implementation. The founder identified under the pseudonym *Satoshi Nakamoto* published in 2008 his white paper describing in detail the bitcoin concept and chose to have it as an open-source project. It became operational from the beginning of 2009 with the help of volunteer programmers.

Fun Fact

The real identity of Satoshi Nakamoto is unknown. He disappeared suddenly from the internet in April 2011 after transferring control of the associated website to other programmers who had helped him and logged off. There has been much speculation as to whether Satoshi is a real person or a group of people behind the pseudonym.

Basics

According to the bitcoin foundation:
Bitcoin is a consensus network that enables a new payment system and a completely digital money. It is the first decentralized peer-to-peer payment network that is

PART 4: The top Coins analyzed.

powered by its users with no central authority or middlemen.[52]

In other words: bitcoin is a cryptocurrency based on a globally distributed blockchain. Its blockchain containing the ledger is updated, and validated by thousands of nodes constantly, making it extremely robust. Nodes get remuneration for supporting the blockchain through users paying transaction fees on top of being eligible for mining rewards.

Bitcoin Mining

Mining bitcoin was a famous way to earn "free" bitcoin. However, it's not true anymore. While miners who win the reward would get 3.125 bitcoin per block, equivalent to $200,000 at the time this book was written. The reward amount is decreasing regularly due to the implemented halving process. Additionally, tough competition has increased to the point that only professional miners with dedicated equipment can make any money out of mining.

Over the years, as Bitcoin gained popularity, it started being accepted in various places as a means of making payments. Two countries gave it increased global recognition by accepting it as an official currency for payments. The first one was El Salvador in 2021, followed by Central African Republic in 2022. In more than a dozens of countries, cryptocurrencies are in use legally for daily payments.⁵³

Advantage

As the 1st cryptocurrency, it is recognized as the dominant one. Usually, when people speak about cryptocurrency, they are referring to bitcoin.

It has the longest existence, and its design and security are seen by many as "proven in use" over the years. Today, more than 18,000 nodes are around the globe, supporting the blockchain making it very reliable.

It is also the most convenient cryptocurrency for beginners as most exchange sites as well as some investment platforms and banks allow you to purchase, transfer, and sell bitcoin directly.

Disadvantage

While aiming to be a payment currency, bitcoin processing speed is not sufficient to replace the credit card payment system as it is.

In addition, like most old cryptocurrencies, the mining process has been criticized for the amount of energy it requires. The most famous voice was that of Tesla inc, which halted accepting it as a means of payment until a viable solution is found.

Evolution

Bitcoin has been slowly evolving but even the most popular cryptocurrency has been suffering due to its limitations. Recently there has been a push to enable an add-on layer on the top of the bitcoin blockchain to enable affordable and much faster transactions. This is known as the lightning network.

The lightning network holds some amount of funds and acts as an automated intermediary for Bitcoin transactions off the chain. All these microtransactions can be done in a very short time with very low fees as only the final settlement is recorded to the Bitcoin blockchain.

Financial

Bitcoin is designed to have 21 million coins, however, as mining is still ongoing there are slightly over 18.8 million Bitcoins in circulation.

Afraid of Losing Money in Cryptocurrencies?

While the recent price is $40,000~$70,000, it is known for large fluctuations. In January 2023, the lowest value was ~$16,000, and the highest was ~$73,000 in March 2024.

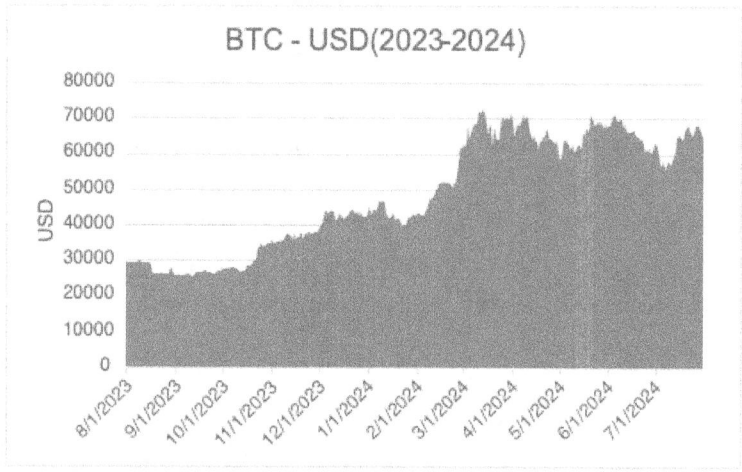

Figure 24: Bitcoin Value In 2023-2024 [54]

Looking over a longer period, the Bitcoin price has increased a lot over the years. For this reason, even if Bitcoin is volatile, investors see it as a long-term investment. It is sometimes even nicknamed the digital gold as it seems unaffected by inflation.

PART 4: The top Coins analyzed.

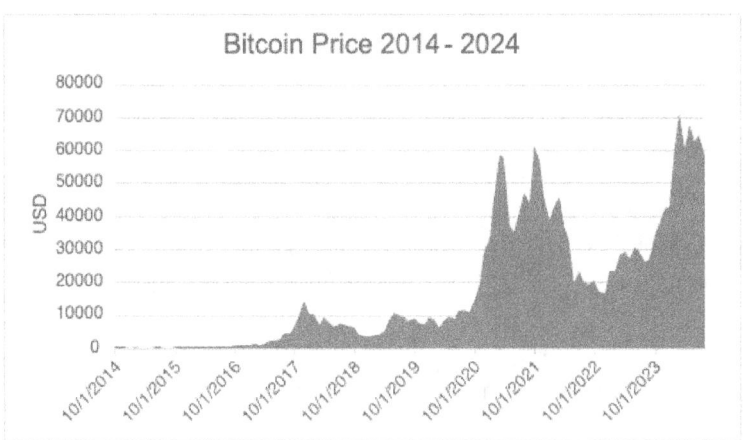

Figure 25: Bitcoin Price Over The Year 2014 -2024 [55]

The increased adoption of bitcoin guides many investors to think its value will keep increasing. Several forecasts predict that bitcoin value to reach news high in 2025:

CoinDCX expects it to hit $100,000[56], and Coinpedia even sees it skyrocketing to a staggering $160,000.[57]

It is important to note that those estimates reflect peak values based on specific market assumptions which can constantly evolve.

To Know More

Official Website	https://bitcoin.org
Whitepaper	https://bitcoin.org/bitcoin.pdf

Afraid of Losing Money in Cryptocurrencies?

Ethereum: The Queen?

Logo	ethereum
Symbol	ETH
Start	2015
Market Value	$317,264,213,000
Rank	#2
Technology level	2nd Generation

DATA AS PER (AUG 2024)

PART 4: The top Coins analyzed.

History

People started realizing blockchain users could do much more than only make payments with blockchain, by using the chain as a distributed computer to run specific programs. Ethereum was the breakthrough to a new generation of cryptocurrencies. Ethereum was initially conceived by Vitalik Buterin in 2013. Thanks to crowdfunding support and multiple co-founders joining in, Ethereum was released in 2015.

Basic

Ethereum came with a framework that allows anyone to make its own blockchain, based on the open ERC20 template. It's very powerful as its ability to integrate code to make smart-contract makes it very polyvalent for many use cases.

The Enterprise Ethereum Alliance today includes hundreds of companies that are using the Ethereum technology and blockchain covering a range of companies from industrial partner Toyota, Samsung, Intel to Software companies such Microsoft and Cisco, and financial institutions like J.P. Morgan and recently Mastercard, and Visa.[58]

Afraid of Losing Money in Cryptocurrencies?

Interesting Fact

In chess, players have a saying: "*A king may be the most important piece on the chessboard, however, the queen is the most powerful*".

Cryptocurrency users can see the same here. The Queen Ethereum brings lots of possibilities that can't be done with the King bitcoin.

Ethereum was not intended to be a cryptocurrency competing with bitcoin but more a complement to it. Still, its token Ether became the second-highest value cryptocurrency as Ether is used to monetize all exchanges and services rendered on the Ethereum blockchain.

Advantage

Ethereum has the most developed digital ecosystem, making it used across many diverse industries. Bloomberg wrote that it's *the hottest platform in the world of cryptocurrencies and blockchains.*[59]

It offers open templates for any actors to set up their own blockchain using the Ethereum standard. This combined with continuous improvements in development allows it to remain a top blockchain.

PART 4: The top Coins analyzed.

Disadvantage

Ethereum also has its flaws. It still has a relatively slow processing speed of 30 operations per second. While this is better than bitcoin it's far from a financial payment standard.

Also, smart-contracts are prone to human error and sometimes hacks. There have been multiple such cases in its 7-year history leading to some hard forks (blockchain and community separation) due to disagreements on how best to fix them. The most famous hard fork led to the creation of the Ethereum Classic (ETC) in 2016.[60]

Evolution

One major update, called Ethereum 2.0, was realized in 2022. Ethereum 2.0 provided a lot of technological improvements to upgrade its blockchain technology from a 2nd generation to a 4th generation cryptocurrency including:

- Switching to a Proof of Stake Consensus

- Sharding: Allowing multiple sub-chains connected to each other to offer scalability.

Afraid of Losing Money in Cryptocurrencies?

Financial

Ethereum has generated over 120,300,000 Ether coins. While there is no maximum cap defined, there has been some proposal to impose a limit of 120 million or 140 million total coin supply. However, in 2021 an update "burning" part of the transaction fees has been rolled out. The burning would safeguard the value of the coin by decreasing the amount of Ethereum coins in circulation over time.

In 2024, the recent price is ~$2,500. As with most of the other cryptocurrencies, it is prone to large fluctuations.

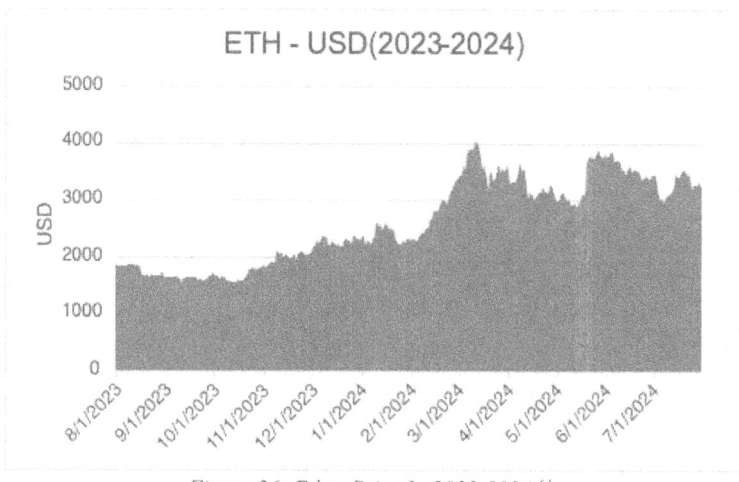

Figure 26: Ether Price In 2023-2024 [61]

In the last 12 months, the lowest value was ~$1,800, and the highest was ~$4,000.

PART 4: The top Coins analyzed.

Looking over a longer period, Ethereum has very good financial potential thanks to its technological evolution. Investors also remarked that together with Bitcoin, Ethereum leads the way in all alt-coin trends.

Figure 27: Ether Price Over The Years 2018-2024 [62]

The increased adoption of Ethereum together with its technological updates gives investors' confidence that the value of Ether will continue to increase.

Multiple forecasts predict that Ether value will reach new highs in coming years:

CoinPriceforecast.com predicted it would reach more than $7,000.[63],and even more optimistic is Cryptonaute.fr which sees it possibly reaching as much as $37,000 in 2030.[64]

Afraid of Losing Money in Cryptocurrencies?

It's important to note that those estimates reflect peak values based on specific market assumptions which can always evolve.

To Know More

Official Website	https://ethereum.org
Whitepaper	https://ethereum.org/what-is-ethereum/

PART 4: The top Coins analyzed.

Binance Coin

Logo	
Coin Symbol	BNB
Start	2017
Market Value	$78,073,526,000
Rank	#4
Technology level	2nd Generation

DATA AS PER (AUG 2024)

Afraid of Losing Money in Cryptocurrencies?

History

Binance Coin is a token issued by the Binance exchange, one of the largest coin exchange platforms. Initially based on Ethereum it later changed to its own blockchain, the Binance smart chain in 2020.

Basics

Its primary use is as a utility token within the Binance exchange platform where it is used to replace transaction fees. Over time, it expanded through partnerships to further usage including credit cards, and also became an investment coin itself.

Advantage

BNB is a very easy coin to buy and sell on the Binance website through a user-friendly interface. Thanks to multiple external partnerships, it has a large ecosystem which makes it useful for more and more purposes. For example, it can be used to buy airline tickets or to pay credit card bills.[65]

PART 4: The top Coins analyzed.

Being used as a key token on one of the most prominent exchange sites gives it a somewhat controlled growth combined with a long-term vision.

Disadvantage

Limited decentralization, i.e., being created and managed by a cryptocurrency exchange means it is not as decentralized and independent as other coins as it has only a few dozen nodes running its blockchain.[66]

Bloomberg reported in past years that Binance Holding is under the scrutiny of the American IRS. While Binance claims it has incorporated tools to detect any fraud using its system, it could impact the value of its coin or its accessibility in some countries.[67]

Financial

Binance coin has generated 200 million BNB coins since its launch. BNB exchanges bring scarcity by burning some BNB they own every quarter. As of today, the total coin offering is down to 168 million BNB Coins.

In 2024 the recent price is ~$550. Like most cryptocurrencies, it is prone to large fluctuations. In the last

Afraid of Losing Money in Cryptocurrencies?

12 months, the lowest value was ~$200, and the highest was ~$700.

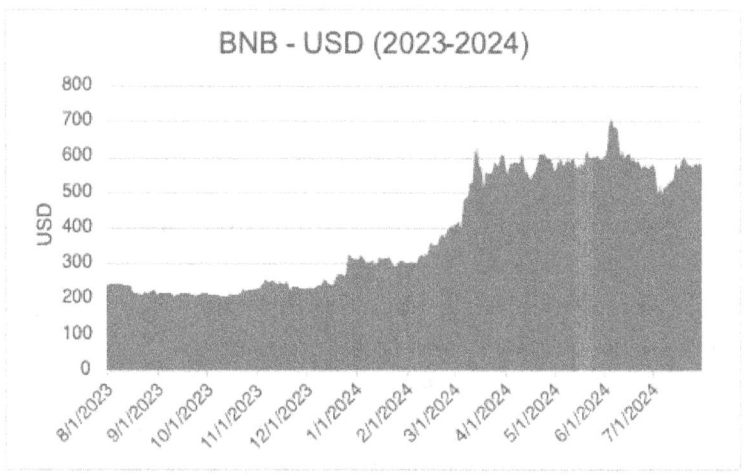

Figure 28: Bnb Price Evolution In 2023-2024 [68]

Looking over a longer period, while its ecosystem became larger, BNB coin value kept increasing. Binance coin has very good financial potential.

PART 4: The top Coins analyzed.

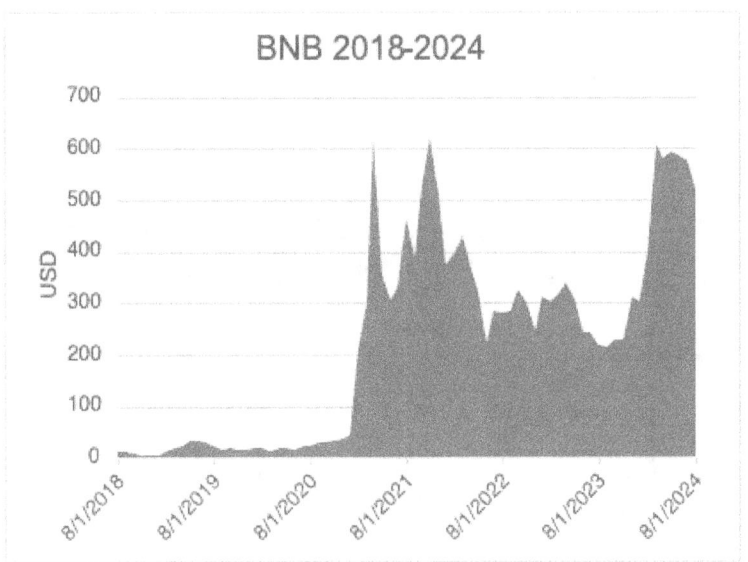

Figure 29: BNB Coin Evolution Over 2018- 2024 [69]

It is possible to believe that the exponential growth phase is already over, and only steady growth can be expected in the future.

walletinvestor.com predicts some growth to a level of $1,000 in 2025.[70] While Cryptonewsz.com sees it growing to in range of $700-$800.[71]

It's important to note that those estimates reflect peak values based on specific market assumptions which may change, especially considering that Binance Exchange actions on the coin could have an impact.

Competition

Several other crypto-exchange platforms have launched their cryptocurrency. Some of the biggest competitors are:

Project	Coin name
Crypto.com Coin	CRO
FTX Token	FTT
Huobi Token	HT

While they are all issued by relatively famous cryptocurrency exchange platforms, none of these coins have yet achieved the success of the Binance coin.

To Know More

Official Website	https://www.binance.org/en#smartChain

PART 4: The top Coins analyzed.

Tether

Logo	tether
Coin Symbol	USDT
Start	2014
Market Value	$116,913,145,000
Rank	#3
Technology level	2nd generation

DATA AS PER (AUG 2024)

Afraid of Losing Money in Cryptocurrencies?

History

Initially launched in 2014 under the name "Realcoin" by co-founders Brock Pierce, Reeve Collins, and Craig Sellars. It was renamed Tether some months later.

Basics

Tether (USDT) is a stablecoin. It means it's designed to prevent volatility which other cryptocurrencies are suffering from. Its value is backed by some amount of USD, keeping the exchange rate close to 1 USDT = 1 USD.

On top of the USDT following the USD, they also provide EUROT aligned on the EURO, and CNHT matching the offshore Chinese yuan (CNH).

Advantage

Stability is the key advantage, investors trading multiple cryptocurrencies, and switching between them can keep their cash balance in Tether to avoid having to convert back to real cash each time. Conversion to a Fiat currency is still a slow process that may take days, whereas storing money in USDT takes only an instant.

PART 4: The top Coins analyzed.

Availability: Tether coins are available on multiple blockchains such as Bitcoin (Omni and Liquid Protocol), Ethereum, EOS, Tron, Algorand, SLP, and OMG blockchains. USDT is also available in most cryptocurrency exchanges.

Disadvantage

Tether is impacted by 2 main controversies. The first one is about its ownership. While Tether is supposed to be managed by the org tether.org, it has been found it was controlled by crypto exchange Bitfinex unofficially as both share executives.[72]

The second one is that Tether suffered from a lawsuit about the USD reserve amount guaranteeing the coin value. Initially, Tether claimed to be 100% backed in real cash reserves, but finally admitted it's a mix of cash, and other financial assets.

This means that if every USDT holder tried to exchange their USDT coin into real USD at the same time, the platform may not be able to cover all transactions completely.[73] While this may sound worrisome to USDT users, it is the same for the banks where we keep regular savings.[74]

Afraid of Losing Money in Cryptocurrencies?

Financial

Tether has generated 76 billion USDT coins since its launch. USDT has no scarcity or limitations, as if a cryptocurrency user buys additional coins, the Tether organization would issue more coins as per market needs to keep it stable.

The stable coin is based on the US dollar, with its value being set at a target of 1 USDT = $1.

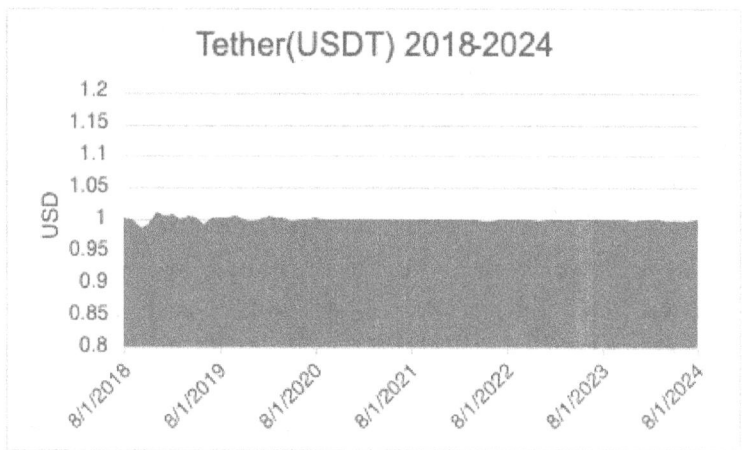

Figure 30: USDT Price Evolution 2018 – 2024 [75]

As a stablecoin, it is known for limited fluctuations. In the last 12 months, the lowest value was ~$0.95, and the highest was ~$1.03.

PART 4: The top Coins analyzed.

Competition

There are other stablecoin like USDT, the biggest competitors are:

Project	Coin name
USD Coin	USDC
DAI	DAI
PayPal USD	PYUSD

To Know More

Official website	https://tether.to/
Whitepaper	https://tether.to/wp-content/uploads/2016/06/TetherWhitePaper.pdf

Afraid of Losing Money in Cryptocurrencies?

Polkadot

Logo	
Coin Symbol	Dot
Start	2020
Market Value	$6,552,598,000
Rank	#15
Technology level	4th generation

DATA AS PER (AUG 2024)

PART 4: The top Coins analyzed.

History

Polkadot was started in 2016 and finally launched openly in 2020. Its main founder is Dr. Gavin Wood who was the former CTO of Ethereum. It was launched to both overcome Ethereum limitations, as well as to support the vision to have a fully decentralized web controlled by its users called *"web 3.0"*.

Basics

Polkadot defines itself as a *"blockchain which unites an entire network of purpose-built blockchains"*.[76] It's a multi-chain network based on proof of stake and sharding technology. Polkadot allows connecting any type of blockchain around a center relay chain.

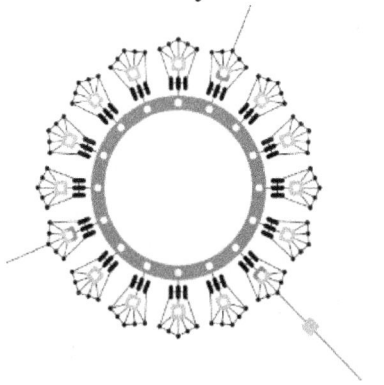

Figure 31: Polkadot Network View [77]

Afraid of Losing Money in Cryptocurrencies?

 The relay chain is the heart of the network. It connects all the sub-chains called parachains together. It's also responsible for maintaining the overall security.

 Parachains design blockchains connected to the relay chain. Each parachain can have its own design and purpose. They can be cryptocurrency chains, smart contract-based chains, or any type of data-sharing blockchain. Parachains have to pay for their connection slot to the Polkadot relay chain using the Dot token.

We can see the Polkadot model as a digital shopping mall building. The Mall lends space for various shops in exchange for rent. All shops share the mall infrastructures as a benefit.

Polkadot also includes bridge blockchain. Bridges are special chains made to connect directly to other blockchain networks such as bitcoin or Ethereum.

Advantage

Scalability: Polkadot brings effective scalability through its multi-chain concept and secure design. It has already attracted many partner chains which are bidding in auctions for one of the 100 connection slots.

PART 4: The top Coins analyzed.

Secure: The bidding process requires that a significant number of coins are locked for the lease duration to prevent scams, and non-serious blockchains from being connected to the network.

Disadvantage

Validation may get controlled by large entities only. The validation concept is limited to the 1,000 largest stakeholders. Only validators able to own 50 to 100 million USD in Dot coin would be eligible. Having a limited number of validators is not really in line with the dream of full decentralization.[78]

Many competitors are trying to do something similar, and even old players such as Ethereum are catching up with their 2.0 upgrade. Whether Polkadot still stays popular with tougher competitions has yet to be seen.

Financial

Polkadot has generated 1.45 billion Dot coins since its launch. Scarcity is increasing as the foundation is burning around 240,000 Dots, they own every month.

Afraid of Losing Money in Cryptocurrencies?

While the recent price is ~$4.5, as most cryptocurrencies, it is prone to large fluctuations. In the last 12 months, the lowest value was ~$3.6, and the highest was ~$11.5.

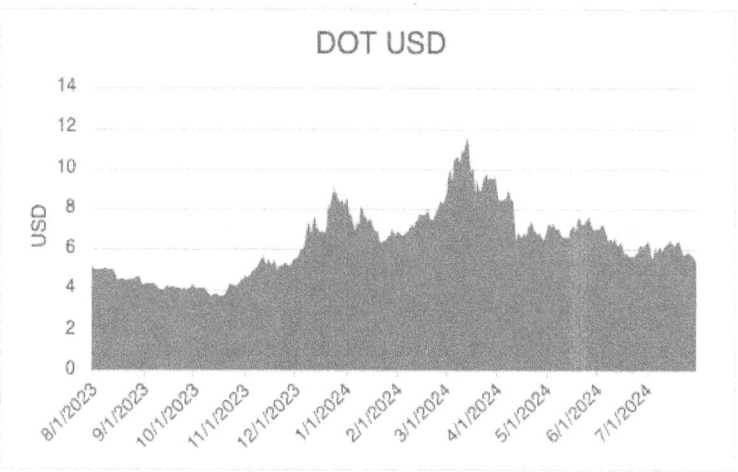

Figure 32: DOT Price In 2023 - 2024[79]

Polkadot, in its 4 years of existence, has already increased considerably in value. The growth being quite in-line with its popularity and new parachain launch, more growth can still be expected.

According to priceprediction.net, Dot will keep growing and reach over $8 in 2025,[80] however, longforecast.com predicts it will be fluctuating around current price in coming years.[81]

It's important to note that those estimates reflect peak values based on specific market assumptions which may change, and also that Polkadot is quite young, where the

PART 4: The top Coins analyzed.

success of the associated parachain will have a strong impact on the Dot value.

Competition

There are other cryptocurrencies similar to Polkadot, some of the biggest competitors are:

Project	Coin name
Avalanche	AVAX
Solana	SOL
Cardano	ADA

There are many more blockchains that are similar to Polkadot as a general & polyvalent network.

To Know More

Official website	https://polkadot.network
Light paper	https://polkadot.network/Polkadot-lightpaper.pdf

Dogecoin

Logo	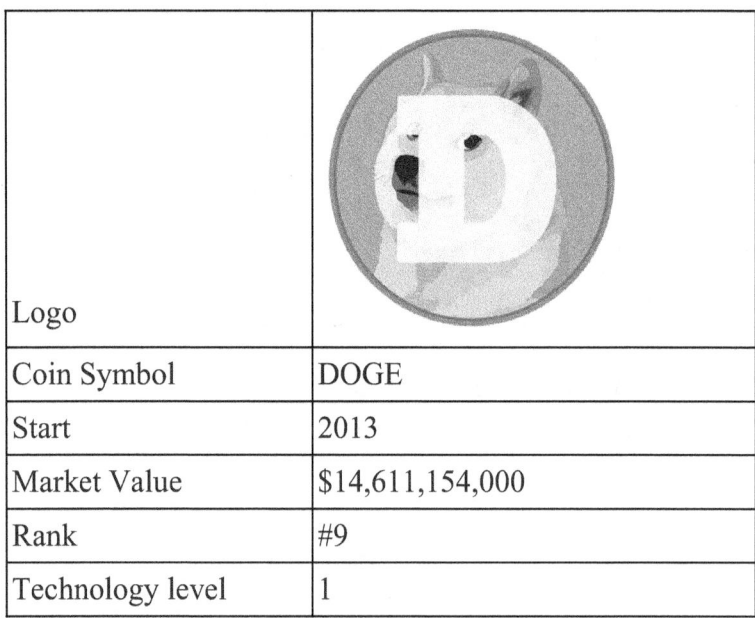
Coin Symbol	DOGE
Start	2013
Market Value	$14,611,154,000
Rank	#9
Technology level	1

DATA AS PER (AUG 2024)

PART 4: The top Coins analyzed.

History

Dogecoin is a cryptocurrency launched in 2013 by Billy Markus and Jackson Palmer. Dogecoin has been managed afterward by the Dogecoin foundation. It is considered the first meme coin and also the most popular one over the years.

Fun Fact

Figure 33: Doge [82]

Dogecoin was started as a kind of joke in opposition to the boom of alt-coin appearing at that time.

Its logo is a Japanese Shiba Inu dog. This dog was in 2013 the top internet Meme picture where people add text to the picture about what the dog is supposedly thinking.

Basics

It is originally based on Litecoin code which itself was modified from Bitcoin code. Dogecoin is a basic cryptocurrency and cannot directly support smart-contract or any advanced blockchain features. The Dogecoin foundation still only plans it to be a form of payment and nothing more.[83]

Advantage

It is one of the few meme coins which has continued to be among the top cryptocurrency coins since its creation. Even if its intrinsic utility is limited; the large user base gives it some value.

Doge being a popular meme coin has higher volatility than most cryptocurrencies giving some of its fans the ability to do short-term (speculative) trading.

Disadvantage

The departure of its co-founder Jakson Palmer in 2015, unhappy to see the dogecoin community only looking for easy enrichment more than the utility left the coin technological development without aims for several years.[84]

Also, Dogecoin users have been suffering multiple times from scams. It is possible that being a meme coin, its users have been less careful than traditional cryptocurrency investors.[85]

PART 4: The top Coins analyzed.

Following its success, many dog themes and other meme coins have spurred. Those meme coins have attracted gambling investors, but most had only limited financial success.

Financial

Dogecoin has generated 145 billion DOGE coins since its launch. Dogecoin can still be mined, and the total coin supply keeps increasing.

In 2024 the recent price is ~$0.1. As a meme coin, it is prone to larger fluctuations than most other cryptocurrencies. In the last 12 months, the lowest value was ~$0.05, and the highest was ~$022.

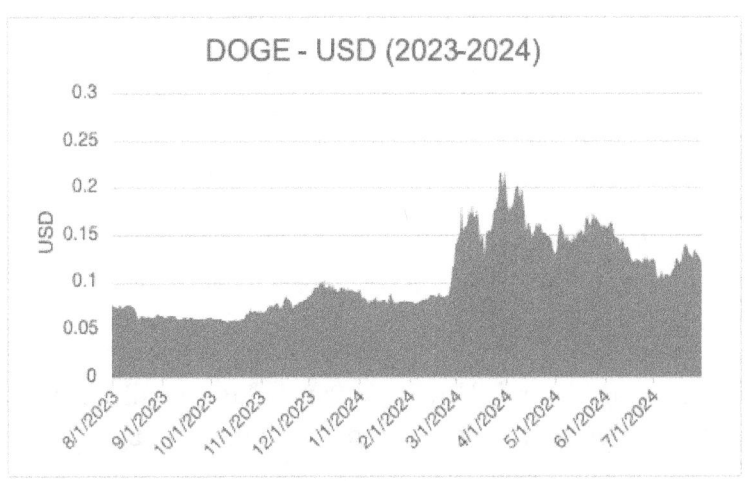

Figure 34: DOGE Price Evolution In 2023-2024 [86]

Afraid of Losing Money in Cryptocurrencies?

Doge had a high fluctuation in 2021, the peak value is equivalent to a fluctuation of approximately 150 times its January value.

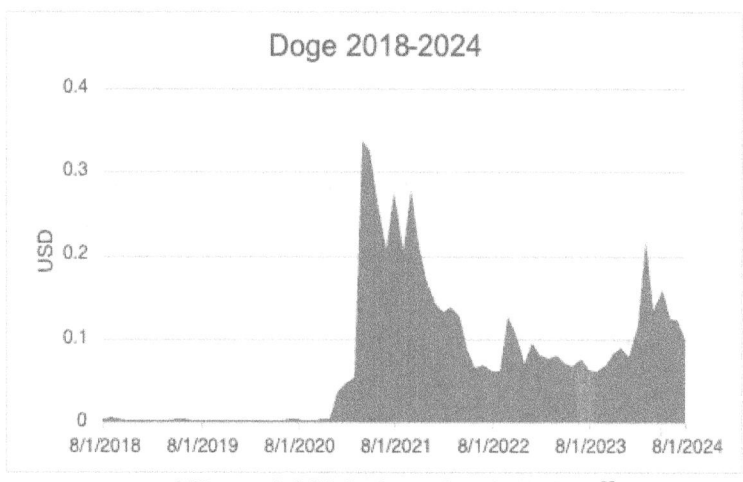

35Figure: DOGE Evolution Over 2018- 2024 [87]

Price predictions don't make sense for meme coins as their value fluctuates based on fan base speculation.

Competition

There are many other meme coins but only one is significant: Shiba INU (SHIB) which has a similar market value to Doge. All others are not worth mentioning.

PART 4: The top Coins analyzed.

To Know More

Official Website	https://dogecoin.com/
Trailmap	https://foundation.dogecoin.com/trailmap/prologue/

Part 5: Non-Fungible Token (NFT)

Part 5: The next crypto crash is coming.

In this book, while we look at most domains related to cryptocurrencies, non-fungible tokens (in short NFT) are a recent addition to the blockchain ecosystem. They have been booming in 2020 & 2021, but the 1st NFT bubble finally crashed in 2022 and are on a pass to become again something better.

Non-Fungible Token in short

NFT is one new functionality based on blockchain technology. They are the exact opposite of cryptocurrencies.

For Bitcoin and other coins, every token is identical. All Bitcoins have the same value and same characteristics. NFTs on the other hand, are designed to be all unique. Since they use Blockchain technology, they are as secure as any cryptocurrency, especially can't be duplicated, and also can be bought and sold similarly.

Several industries are starting to use it, especially in the artistic field, as NFT allows to perfectly traces the authenticity of an item. When a digital artist sells a drawing as NFT, the buyer can be sure of getting the original. In this way, a middleman such as an art gallery may not be required anymore. Wine collectors started using it to label physical bottles to ensure traceability of their origin.[88]

The problem with NFT

NFT seems good for logistics use cases and perfect for collectors. If it stayed there it would be fine, however, it is plagued with low-quality digital pieces of art which can be created by millions by automated scripts and greedy investors looking to make money on hype.

One famous example of the excess with NFT is the  EtheRock. A series of 100 digital pictures of a (simple) rock. These pictures started to have their price increases to over a million USD each during summer 2021.[89]

The publisher of these pictures does clearly state *"These virtual rocks serve NO PURPOSE beyond being able to be bought and sold"* [90]

NFT reaching such prices without valid justification is a sign cryptocurrencies market has a problem.

Part 5: The next crypto crash is coming.

NFT are a risky and bad investment

Collector versus investment

Collectors are professionals which are willing to put a price to acquire a piece of art or specific rare items.

When King Francis I acquired the Mona Lisa painting [91] from Leonardo da Vinci, he knew he truly wanted that painting for himself. He was willing to pay a high price for it to keep it. He did not buy it as an investment, hoping the painting value would increase later.

Figure 36: Mona Lisa

In a similar way, there are collectors for many rare items such as old stamps, Japanese character dolls, or Baseball trading cards. Collectors want these rare items to complete their collection. They would keep them and only sometimes look to resell them.

Investors need to be aware that collectible items are an extremely risky investment, with only a niche market. Estimating the right price for an artwork requires usually being an expert. Additionally, if the collectible goes out of fashion, they may lose all their value. The baseball card market which was strong in 20's century has shrunk a lot in

Afraid of Losing Money in Cryptocurrencies?

interest, and some may remember the Pogs from the mid-'90s which are essentially not worth anything anymore.[92]

The 1st NFT crash

According to the market research by coin telegraph, the total spent amount on NFT increased from ~$40 million in 2018 to over $17 billion in 2021.[93] A part of it may be due to collectors buying rare pieces of art or collectible goods, still many NFTs are being bought by short-sighted investors looking to make quick money on hysteria. With these initial investors giving some profit, and with a strong FOMO effect, more and more investors are jumping on thousands of valueless items in the hope of profit. Sellers are also encouraging it by releasing larger collections of NFTs thanks to AI being able to create thousands of variations of an item in seconds.[94]

As of the end of 2021, the NFTs were equivalent to 1% of the total cryptocurrency market. This uncontrolled growth formed an NFT bubble which exploded abruptly losing majority of its value. in 2024 NFTGo evaluated fluctuating bet 4 and 10 billion USD.[95]

Part 5: The next crypto crash is coming.

NFT impact on cryptocurrencies market

One of the key reasons for the 2008 financial crisis was the housing price bubble in the USA. Some investors were buying overpriced houses, hoping to sell them later at even higher prices. When the bubble collapsed it undermined the complete financial market as housing loans were connected to many other investments.[96]

In a comparable way, the explosion of an NFT bubble impacted severely the cryptocurrency market. A sudden drop in the values of all NFTs created a liquidity crunch when everyone tried to salvage part of their failed investment. This snowball into an avalanche which can take down the price of all NFTs and cryptocurrencies.

The "2018 Great Crypto Crash" saw the market loses over 80% of its value between January and November of that year.[97] History could repeat itself, Cryptocurrency thanks to its diversified utility has recover from this crash again, but NFTs may have less chance to rise very high again.

NFT market restart

In 2024, NFT market has matured with more responsible usage of NFT. Several consumer brands have entered the market offering unique NFTs as part of their brand

Afraid of Losing Money in Cryptocurrencies?

communication, online games started to use NFTs too for special assets and goodies.

Still NFTs should not be considered as an investment since goodies items does not have logical but only emotional value.

Conclusion

While cryptocurrencies may be a good long-term investment, it has significant risk. Investors need to be aware and research carefully before entering it.

I hope this book helps you on the crypto journey. Remember the wisest advice is *Investors should not invest more than they can afford to lose!*

Acknowledgement

Writing a book is harder than I thought, and I would have never made it without help.

I have to start by thanking my awesome wife, Mariko. She has always been next to me in all the good things I ever accomplished in my life, including this book.

I want to thank Israel Heber Hernandez Garcia, my long-time best friend. He has been continuously supporting me in writing the book. Always picky in improving my writing quality and readability.

I want to thank my British friend Craig Hills. Thanks to him, for the 900+ correction points he made. Without him, this book would be broken in Frenglish. The English sentences are now readable.

I want to thank Praveen Shivappa-Shastry, my office colleague. He spent a good time reviewing the style and gave insightful readability comments.

The cover page is the amazing design of Sushmita Selvadass, As most people judge a book by its cover, she gave it a real nice professional look.

One more special thanks to Rubia Ragavan, which helped me finish this book.

I want to thank all the other friends who gave me hints and advice along the journey.

I want to thank the amazing MBA Quantic School of Business and Technology for daring to include modern classes such as blockchain. Without it, I may have never gone on the journey to learn more about cryptocurrency.

Finally, I want to thank God. *"I can do all this through him who gives me strength. Philippians 4:13, NIV"*

Afraid of Losing Money in Cryptocurrencies?

Citations & Reference

No book would be complete without its sources.
Note: All links have been crosschecked in August 2024

Foreword Works Cited

[1] Hyatt, John. Decoding Crypto: The 10 Most Popular Cryptocurrencies. https://www.nasdaq.com/articles/decoding-crypto%3A-the-10-most-popular-cryptocurrencies-2021-08-05. Accessed 8 Nov. 2021.

[2] Kingsland - School of Blockchain. "94% of Fortune 500 Execs Have Blockchain Project Plans — Do You?" Kingsland University, 24 Sept. 2018, https://medium.com/kingsland/94-of-fortune-500-execs-have-blockchain-project-plans-do-you-15d27d4c5b3d.

[3] "Crypto." Visa, https://usa.visa.com/solutions/crypto.html. Accessed 8 Nov. 2021.

Part 1 Works Cited

[4] Contributors to Wikimedia projects. "SHA-2." Wikipedia, 20 Oct. 2021, https://en.wikipedia.org/wiki/SHA-2.

[5] "Dogecoin USD (DOGE-USD) Price, News, Quote & History." Yahoo Finance, https://finance.yahoo.com/quote/DOGE-USD/history?p=DOGE-USD. Accessed 9 Nov. 2021.

[6] Research, Schwab Center for Financial. "Market Correction: What Does It Mean?" Schwab Brokerage, https://www.schwab.com/learn/story/market-correction-what-does-it-mean. Accessed 18 Aug. 2024.

Citations & Reference

[7] Bitcoin: A Peer-to-Peer Electronic Cash System. https://bitcoin.org/en/bitcoin-paper. Accessed 9 Nov. 2021.

[8] "File:Cryptocurrency Mining Equipment.Jpg." Wikimedia Commons, 19 Apr. 2021, https://commons.wikimedia.org/wiki/File:Cryptocurrency_Mining_Equipment.jpg.

[9] Huang, Jon, et al. "Bitcoin Uses More Electricity Than Many Countries. How Is That Possible?" The New York Times, 3 Sept. 2021, https://www.nytimes.com/interactive/2021/09/03/climate/bitcoin-carbon-footprint-electricity.html.

[10] "No, Visa Doesn't Handle 24,000 TPS and Neither Does Your Pet Blockchain – Blockchain Bitcoin News." Bitcoin News, 20 Apr. 2018, https://news.bitcoin.com/no-visa-doesnt-handle-24000-tps-and-neither-does-your-pet-blockchain/.

[11] "Ethereum Whitepaper." Ethereum, https://ethereum.org/en/whitepaper/. Accessed 10 Nov. 2021.

[12] "File:Vending Machine in Finland.Jpg." Wikimedia Commons, 23 June 2019, https://commons.m.wikimedia.org/wiki/File:Vending_machine_in_Finland.jpg.

[13] etherscan.io. "Ethereum Daily Transactions Chart." Ethereum (ETH) Blockchain Explorer, https://etherscan.io/chart/tx. Accessed 10 Nov. 2021.

[14] News, BBC. "CryptoKitties Craze Slows down Transactions on Ethereum." BBC News, 5 Dec. 2017, https://www.bbc.com/news/technology-42237162.

[15] "File:Proof of Stake.Png." Wikimedia Commons, 6 June 2018, https://commons.wikimedia.org/wiki/File:Proof_of_stake.png.

[16] Contributors to Wikimedia projects. "Lightning Network." Wikipedia, 8 Nov. 2021, https://en.wikipedia.org/wiki/Lightning_Network.

[17] "The Eth2 Upgrades." Ethereum, https://ethereum.org/en/eth2/. Accessed 10 Nov. 2021.

Part 2 Works cited

Afraid of Losing Money in Cryptocurrencies?

[18] CNBC Press Release. "CNBC Transcript: Billionaire Investors Warren Buffett & Charlie Munger Sit Down with CNBC's Becky Quick for CNBC's 'Buffett & Munger: A Wealth of Wisdom.'" CNBC, 30 June 2021, https://www.cnbc.com/2021/06/29/cnbc-transcript-billionaire-investors-warren-buffett-charlie-munger-sit-down-with-cnbcs-becky-quick-for-cnbcs-buffett-munger-a-wealth-of-wisdom-.html.

[19] "Fiat Money." Encyclopedia Britannica, https://www.britannica.com/topic/fiat-money. Accessed 23 Nov. 2021.

[20] Money: At the Center of Transactions. https://www.imf.org/external/pubs/ft/fandd/basics/26-money.htm. Accessed 23 Nov. 2021.

[21] "CryptoCurrency Price." Gold Price, https://goldprice.org/cryptocurrency-price. Accessed 24 Aug. 2024.

[22] "Historical Snapshot - 05 May 2013." CoinMarketCap, https://coinmarketcap.com/historical/20130505/. Accessed 23 Nov. 2021.

[23] "All Cryptocurrencies." CoinMarketCap, https://coinmarketcap.com/all/views/all/. Accessed 19 Aug. 2024.

[24] "Check Cryptocurrency Price History For The Top Coins." CoinMarketCap, https://coinmarketcap.com/historical/. Accessed 25 Aug. 2024.

[25] Reiff, Nathan. "Why Bitcoin Price Predictions Are Unreliable." *Investopedia*, 20 Nov. 2021, https://www.investopedia.com/tech/why-bitcoin-price-predictions-are-unreliable/.

[26] Tchir, Peter. "Paying Attention To The Incentives Of Bitcoin Pundits." *Forbes*, 30 June 2018, https://www.forbes.com/sites/petertchir/2018/06/30/the-never-ending-stream-of-fake-news-in-bitcoin/?sh=7c82765f2dd3.

[27] Biggs, John. "How to Price Cryptocurrencies." TechCrunch, 22 Jan. 2018, https://techcrunch.com/2018/01/22/how-to-price-cryptocurrencies/.

[28] "Cryptocurrency Prices, Charts And Market Capitalizations." CoinMarketCap, https://coinmarketcap.com/. Accessed 16 Dec. 2021.

[29] News, BBC. "Squid Game Crypto Token Collapses in Apparent Scam." *BBC News*, 2 Nov. 2021, https://www.bbc.com/news/business-59129466.

Citations & Reference

[30] Landau, Shira. "DeFi Cryptocurrency Rug Pulls." CyberTalk, 2 Sept. 2021, https://www.cybertalk.org/2021/09/02/defi-cryptocurrency-rug-pulls/.

Part 3 Works cited

[31] Newbery, Emma. "Why Crypto.Com Coin (CRO) Is Up Over 180% in a Month." *The Ascent by The Motley Fool*, 18 Nov. 2021, https://www.fool.com/the-ascent/cryptocurrency/articles/why-cryptocom-coin-cro-is-up-over-180-in-a-month/.

[32] "File:Candlestick Chart in MetaTrader 5.Png." Wikimedia Commons, 17 Oct. 2019, https://commons.wikimedia.org/wiki/File:Candlestick_Chart_in_MetaTrader_5.png.

[33] Kahneman, Daniel, et al. Noise: A Flaw in Human Judgment. Little, Brown Spark, 2021.

[34] "Here's How Much of Your Investing Portfolio Should Be in Crypto, According to 5 Experts." NextAdvisor, 21 May 2021, https://time.com/nextadvisor/investing/cryptocurrency/how-much-your-portfolio-should-be-crypto/.

[35] Housel, Morgan. The Psychology of Money: Timeless Lessons on Wealth, Greed, and Happiness. Harriman House Limited, 2020.

[36] Definition of Herd Mentality. https://www.merriam-webster.com/dictionary/herd%20mentality. Accessed 28 Dec. 2021.

[37] Žiga Vižintin. "Why Five and Not Eight? How Round Number Bias Can Reduce Your Nest Egg." Behavioral Scientist, 7 Feb. 2018, https://behavioralscientist.org/five-not-eight-round-number-bias-can-reduce-nest-egg/.

[38] "Cardano USD (ADA-USD) Price, Value, News & History." Yahoo Finance, https://finance.yahoo.com/quote/ADA-USD. Accessed 28 Dec. 2021.

[39] Ph.D., Gary Klein. "The Curious Case of Confirmation Bias." Psychology Today, 5 May 2019, https://www.psychologytoday.com/us/blog/seeing-what-others-dont/201905/the-curious-case-confirmation-bias

Afraid of Losing Money in Cryptocurrencies?

[40] Delfabbro, Paul, et al. "Cryptocurrency Trading, Gambling and Problem Gambling." Addictive Behaviors, vol. 122, Nov. 2021, p. 107021, https://doi.org/10.1016/j.addbeh.2021.107021.

[41] Guglielmo, Riccardo, et al. "Is Pathological Trading an Overlooked Form of Addiction?" Addiction & Health, vol. 8, no. 3, July 2016, pp. 207–09.

[42] Fong, Timothy W. "The Biopsychosocial Consequences of Pathological Gambling." Psychiatry (Edgmont (Pa.□: Township)), vol. 2, no. 3, Mar. 2005, pp. 22–30.

[43] BITO. https://www.proshares.com/our-etfs/strategic/bito. Accessed 21 Dec. 2021.

[44] The SEC has approved bitcoin ETFs. https://www.theguardian.com/technology/2024/jan/11/bitcoin-etf-approved-sec-explained-meaning-securities-regulator-tweet
Accessed 21 Sep. 2024.

[45] EToro, https://www.etoro.com/smartportfolios/thetie-longonly. Accessed 21 Dec. 2021.

[46] "Multi Crypto AI @Napoleon-X CopyPortfolio." EToro, https://www.etoro.com/smartportfolios/napoleon-x. Accessed 21 Dec. 2021.

[47] "Montana - Power Block Coin to Build $251M Data Center to Mine Crypto." NewsBTC, 22 Feb. 2018, https://www.newsbtc.com/news/bitcoin/montana-power-block-coin-llc-to-build-251-million-data-center-to-mine-cryptocurrency/.

[48] "File:Cryptocurrency Mining Farm.Jpg." Wikimedia Commons, 27 May 2015, https://commons.wikimedia.org/wiki/File:Cryptocurrency_Mining_Farm.jpg.

[49] "Ethereum 2.0 FAQ." ConsenSys, https://consensys.net/knowledge-base/ethereum-2/faq/. Accessed 16 Dec. 2021.

[50] "Earn Crypto Rewards with Binance ETH 2.0 Staking." Binance, https://www.binance.com/en/eth2. Accessed 16 Dec. 2021.

[51] Tidy, By Joe. "Bitcoin: Fake Elon Musk Giveaway Scam 'Cost Man

Citations & Reference

£400,000.'" *BBC News*, 16 Mar. 2021, https://www.bbc.com/news/technology-56402378.

Part 4 Works cited

[52] "FAQ." Bitcoin, https://bitcoin.org/en/faq. Accessed 14 Dec. 2021.

[53] Countries Where Bitcoin Is Legal and Illegal, Investopedia.com https://www.investopedia.com/articles/forex/041515/countries-where-bitcoin-legal-illegal.asp

[54] "Bitcoin USD (BTC-USD) Price, Value, News & History." Yahoo Finance, https://finance.yahoo.com/quote/BTC-USD/. Accessed 19 Aug. 2024.

[55] "Bitcoin USD (BTC-USD) Price, Value, News & History." Yahoo Finance, https://finance.yahoo.com/quote/BTC-USD/. Accessed 19 Aug. 2024.

[56] https://coindcx.com/blog/price-predictions/bitcoin-price-weekly/ Accessed 1 Sep. 2024

[57] Bitcoin Price Prediction 2024 – 2030, 1 Sep 2024, https://coinpedia.org/price-prediction/bitcoin-price-prediction/.

[58] entethalliance. "EEA MEMBERS." Enterprise Ethereum Alliance, 11 Apr. 2018, https://entethalliance.org/eea-members/.

[59] Kharif, Olga. "Bitcoin's Top Rival Is Up 90% and Ready to Ditch Mining." Bloomberg, 28 Feb. 2017, https://www.bloomberg.com/news/articles/2017-02-28/bitcoin-s-top-rival-is-up-90-and-readying-its-next-big-move.

[60] "ETC vs. ETH: Ethereum Classic's Ideological Rift." Gemini, https://www.gemini.com/cryptopedia/ethereum-classic-etc-vs-eth#section-ethereum-vs-ethereum-classic. Accessed 14 Dec. 2021.

[61] "Ethereum USD (ETH-USD) Price, Value, News & History." Yahoo Finance, https://finance.yahoo.com/quote/ETH-USD/. Accessed 19 Aug. 2024.

[62] "Ethereum USD (ETH-USD) Price, Value, News & History." Yahoo Finance, https://finance.yahoo.com/quote/ETH-USD/. Accessed 19 Aug. 2024.

Afraid of Losing Money in Cryptocurrencies?

[63] Coin Price Forecast. "ETHEREUM PRICE PREDICTION 2021 - 2025 - 2030." 01 Sep 2024, https://coinpriceforecast.com/ethereum-forecast-2020-2025-2030.

[64] Ethereum : cours et prédiction prix (2023 – 2024-2025) Cryptonaute, 01 Sep. 2024, https://cryptonaute.fr/ethereum-prediction-2022-2030/.

[65] "#UseBNB: Get Free BNB on Bitcoin Rewards + Book a Flight on TravelbyBit With BNB." Binance Blog, https://www.binance.com/en/blog/all/usebnb-get-free-bnb-on-bitcoin-rewards-+-book-a-flight-on-travelbybit-with-bnb-345799565042417664. Accessed 16 Dec. 2021.

[66] Lukas, Kolin. "How to Use Binance Smart Chain (BSC) for Beginners - Kolin Lukas." Medium, 11 May 2021, https://kolinlukasx.medium.com/how-to-use-binance-smart-chain-bsc-for-beginners-7db971259d80.

[67] "Bloomberg." Are You a Robot?, https://www.bloomberg.com/news/articles/2021-05-13/binance-probed-by-u-s-as-money-laundering-tax-sleuths-bore-in. Accessed 21 Dec. 2021.

[68] "BinanceCoin USD (BNB-USD) Price, Value, News & History." Yahoo Finance, https://finance.yahoo.com/quote/BNB-USD/. Accessed 19 Aug. 2024.

[69] "BinanceCoin USD (BNB-USD) Price, Value, News & History." Yahoo Finance, https://finance.yahoo.com/quote/BNB-USD/. Accessed 19 Aug. 2024.

[70] "Binance Coin Price Prediction: Up to $1001.790! - BNB to USD Forecast 2024, Long-Term & Short-Term Price Prognosis." Walletinvestor.Com, https://walletinvestor.com/forecast/binance-coin-prediction. Accessed 1 sep. 2024.

[71] "CryptoNewsZ." CryptoNewsZ, 1 sep. 2024, https://www.cryptonewsz.com/forecast/binance-coin-price-prediction/.

[72] Lyons, Kim. "Tether Will Pay $41 Million over 'Misleading' Claims It Was Fully Backed by US Dollars." The Verge, 15 Oct. 2021,

[73] Markovich, Sarit. "Commentary: The Overlooked Actor That Could Crash Bitcoin." Fortune, 5 Dec. 2017, https://fortune.com/2017/12/05/bitcoin-btc-price-usd-tether-limited-bitfinex/

Citations & Reference

[74] Contributors to Wikimedia projects. "Bank Reserves." Wikipedia, 24 Sept. 2021, https://en.wikipedia.org/wiki/Bank_reserves#Cash_held_by_banks.

[75] "Tether USD (USDT-USD) Price, Value, News & History." Yahoo Finance, https://finance.yahoo.com/quote/USDT-USD/. Accessed 19 Aug. 2024.

[76] An Introduction to Polkadot, https://polkadot.network/Polkadot-lightpaper.pdf. Accessed 13 Nov. 2021.

[77] An Introduction to Polkadot, https://polkadot.network/Polkadot-lightpaper.pdf. Accessed 13 Nov. 2021.

[78] "Here's Why Polkadot Will Fail?" ProVsCons, https://provscons.com/heres-why-polkadot-will-fail/. Accessed 13 Nov. 2021.

[79] "Polkadot USD (DOT1-USD) Price, Value, News & History." Yahoo Finance, https://finance.yahoo.com/quote/DOT-USD/. Accessed 30 Aug. 2024.

[80] "Polkadot Price Prediction 2022, 2025, 2030." Https://Priceprediction.Net, https://priceprediction.net/en/price-prediction/polkadot. Accessed 01 Sep. 2024.

[81] "POLKADOT PRICE PREDICTION 2021, 2022-2025." Long Forecast, https://longforecast.com/polkadot. Accessed 01 Sep. 2024.

[82] "So Wallpaper, So Doge." Flickr, https://www.flickr.com/photos/flyingblogspot/11025069063. Accessed 27 Dec. 2021.

[83] Foundation], map[name:Dogecoin. Dogecoin Trailmap: Prologue. 10 Dec. 2021, https://foundation.dogecoin.com/trailmap/prologue/.

[84] Murphy, Mike. "Dogecoin Co-Creator Blasts Crypto as a Scam to Help the Rich Get Richer." MarketWatch, 15 July 2021, https://www.marketwatch.com/story/dogecoin-co-creator-blasts-crypto-as-a-scam-to-help-the-rich-get-richer-11626310808.

[85] Gerard, David. "Dogecoin Started as a Joke and Became a Scam." Foreign Policy, 11 Feb. 2021, https://foreignpolicy.com/2021/02/11/dogecoin-how-does-it-work-elon-musk-cryptocurrency/.

Afraid of Losing Money in Cryptocurrencies?

---

[86] "Dogecoin USD (DOGE-USD) Price, Value, News & History." Yahoo Finance, https://finance.yahoo.com/quote/DOGE-USD/. Accessed 19 Aug. 2024.

[87] "Dogecoin USD (DOGE-USD) Price, Value, News & History." Yahoo Finance, https://finance.yahoo.com/quote/DOGE-USD/. Accessed 19 Aug. 2024.

Part 5 Works cited

[88] Makrygiannis, Konstantinos. "EY Helps WiV Technology Accelerate Fine Wine Investing with Blockchain." *EY*, 12 Aug. 2019, https://www.ey.com/en_gl/news/2019/08/ey-helps-wiv-technology-accelerate-fine-wine-investing-with-blockchain.

[89] "Man of Many." *Man of Many*, 30 Aug. 2021, https://manofmany.com/entertainment/art/jpeg-nft-rock-sells-1-7-million.

[90] *Ether Rock*. https://etherrock.com/. Accessed 2 Jan. 2022.

[91] "File:Mona Lisa.Jpg." *Wikipedia*, https://en.wikipedia.org/wiki/File:Mona_Lisa.jpg. Accessed 2 Jan. 2022.

[92] India, Business Insider. "21 Collector's Items That Are Actually Worthless Today." *Business Insider India*, 29 Oct. 2019, https://www.businessinsider.in/slideshows/miscellaneous/21-collectors-items-that-are-actually-worthless-today/slidelist/71808496.cms#slideid=71808497.

[93] Research, Cointelegraph. "NFT Sales Aim for a $17.7B Record in 2021: Report by Cointelegraph Research." *Cointelegraph*, 30 Nov. 2021, https://cointelegraph.com/news/nft-sales-aim-for-a-17-7b-record-in-2021-report-by-cointelegraph-research.

[94] "NFT Generator." *Hotpot.Ai*, https://hotpot.ai/nft-generator?s=footer. Accessed 2 Jan. 2022.

[95] NFT market analysis by NFTgo, 07 Sept. 2024, https://nftgo.io/macro/market-overview.

[96] https://www.britannica.com/event/financial-crisis-of-2007-2008

Citations & Reference

[97] "Bitcoin Continues Steep Fall as Cryptocurrency Collapse Worsens." *The Wall Street Journal*, 26 Nov. 2018, https://www.wsj.com/articles/bitcoin-falls-below-4-000-as-cryptocurrency-collapse-worsens-1543241154.

www.ingramcontent.com/pod-product-compliance
Lightning Source LLC
Chambersburg PA
CBHW071407210526
45465CB00001B/290